HOw
DO
YOU
MEASURE
UP?

All your measuring
and weighing questions answered

Shirley Bond

How Do You Measure Up

© Shirley Bond 2011

Published by Woodlands Publishing

www.woodlandspublishing.co.uk

All rights reserved.

ISBN 978-0-9558911-2-0

Prepared, printed and distributed by:

York Publishing Services Ltd,
64 Hallfield Road,
Layerthorpe,
York
YO31 7ZQ

Tel: 01904 431213

www.yps-publishing.co.uk

To order copies of this book please visit www.ypd-books.com

CONTENTS

Chapter 8 Cooking

Chapter 9 Small cooking equipment

Chapter 10 Large cooking equipment

Chapter 11 Measuring food for energy

ABOUT THE AUTHOR

Shirley Bond is a qualified Nutritionist, State Registered Dietitian and Home Economist.

After working for several years as a dietitian in hospitals she became a lecturer on food and nutrition for the Flour Advisory Bureau in London.

Since her marriage she has worked as a freelance author writing on food and nutrition.

She has written several books, numerous articles for magazines and newspapers and is a regular contributer of articles and recipes to web sites.

She is particularly keen on encouraging people to prepare and cook healthy food at home.

It is this work which has made her very aware of the great confusion caused by the problems with measuring, especially in the kitchen.

It is to help everyone around the world out of this muddle that this book is written.

HERE IS YOUR ONE STOP SOURCE OF INFORMATION FOR SUCCESS IN MEASURING AND WEIGHING ESPECIALLY IN THE KITCHEN

What a muddle there is in the weights and measures used today, especially in the home and more especially in the kitchen.

Recipe books hold a fascination for many people and most homes have quite a collection. They range from the large, beautifully illustrated 'coffee table' type book which is read, enjoyed and inspirational, to cheaper more practical books. Recipe sections in magazines and on web sites are written for everyday reference by those who need guidance when cooking and want to add variety and nutritional value to their meals. And then there are very old housecraft books and collections of recipes written in note books and on scraps of paper lovingly handed down through the generations. It will be a great pity if old family and traditional recipes are no longer enjoyed just because the measures given cannot be understood or interpreted. Also it is a great shame if new recipes written in metric measures are not used because the ingredients are written in a way with which the cook is not familiar.

Any book published in Britain before the mid to late 1960's will have ingredients, oven temperatures and sizes of cooking equipment listed only in Imperial measures. Very old recipes often just suggest adding a handful or a pinch of something instead of a measurement. In the past, the required temperature of the cooker was usually only given in degrees Fahrenheit or Gas mark, or the recipe might only suggest 'cook in a moderate oven'. So although many measures in new recipes in Britain are now given in metric measures, there are many situations where it is essential to be able to convert any recipe to whichever method of measuring and cooking you prefer and understand.

Confusion can be caused by there being two and sometimes three measures given alongside each ingredient. Some recipe writers choose to write Imperial measures first followed by the metric measures in brackets. Others give the metric measure first and the Imperial in brackets. Many also add the American or Australian cup equivalents. This can lead to the belief that the three kinds of measure alongside each ingredient are equal which usually they are not. If they are made equal by doing a mathematical exercise then the recipe will look very odd and be difficult to measure as there will be odd grams and/or fractions of ounces used. The main thing to remember is to follow the same set of measures all through and not to begin weighing some ingredients out in metric and then switching to Imperial or cups or vice versa. The recipe may work but may well not. If several types of measure are given, the recipe should have been tested each way before printing and so should work whichever method of measuring you choose to use, but this is not always done.

Everyone likes entertaining, so guidance on portion sizes for many foods are included, measures to make and cook a few standard recipes and the freezing of items such as sandwiches. For food safety, guidance for the use and temperature of refrigerators, freezers and cookers is given.

Shopping can be a problem unless labelling is understood, so help with this is included.

To enjoy American and Australian recipes in which the ingredients are mostly listed in cups, conversion to Imperial or metric quantities may also be required.

Australian recipes vary from those in the United Kingdom as the ounce is taken as equivalent to 30 g whereas in Britain it is taken as equivalent to 25 g. So care needs to be taken when converting Australian recipes to metric measures or vice versa. Standard equipment like measuring cups and even a pint measure vary in capacity between Australia, the USA and Britain.

Some books and magazines include a conversion chart but many of these have been found to be unreliable, resulting in mistakes being made and the recipe not being a success. This is wasteful besides being disappointing. Some information on measurements is available on some web sites but most of that is not written for practical use in the kitchen.

One other item related to food has been included. This is information on calories/kilocalories and joules/kilojoules for health and body weight control.

Thousands of people every day have to cope with shopping and cooking. As recipes are now shared around the world it is to help everyone out of all this confusion that this book is written.

CHAPTER 1

STANDARD ABBREVIATIONS AND SYMBOLS

Before looking at actual measurements and their equivalents, this chapter gives the standard abbreviations and symbols used instead of the name of the measurement being written in full. This will be helpful to **everyone** and prevent mistakes occurring in many fields. For instance if the mile is carelessly abbreviated to 'm' (incorrect) it can be confused with 'm' meaning metre which is correct. In America the mile is often shortened to 'mi' but in the UK the mile should always be written in full as 'mile'.

It can be seen from the list below that except for the symbols for units of power, for instance the watt can be written 'W' and degrees Celsius written °C, all abbreviations and symbols use lower case, that is small letters.

When writing abbreviations do not put a full stop after them, for instance cm not cm. even at the end of a sentence. If you are writing a metric measurement in full and in plural then add an 's', for instance centimetres.

If you are writing an abbreviation then do not add an 's' when writing a plural, for instance 'cm' not 'cms'.

acre	acre	cubic inch	cu in or in^3
		cubic kilometre	km^3
bar	bar	cubic metre	m^3
		cubic mile	mi^3
centilitre	cl	cubic millimetre	mm^3
centimetre	cm	cubic yard	yd^3
cubic centimetre	cm^3	degree Celsius	°C
cubic foot	cu ft or ft^3	dozen	doz

foot or feet	ft	millimetre	mm
feet per second	ft/s	millisecond	ms
		minute	min
gallon	gal	ounce	oz
gigawatt	GW		
gram	g	pint	pt
hectare	ha	pound	lb
hour	hr		
hundredweight	cwt	quart	qt
inch	in	second	s
		square centimetre	cm²
kilogram	kg	square foot	ft²
kilometre	km	square inch	in²
kilometres per hour	km/h	square kilometre	km²
kilowatt	kW	square metre	m²
		square mile	sq mile
litre	l	square millimetre	mm²
		square yard	yd²
megawatt	MW		
metre	m	tablespoon	tbsp
metres per second	m/s	teaspoon	tsp
mile	mi	ton	ton
millibar	mbar	tonne	t or tonne
milligram	mg		
millilitre	ml	watt	W
	(sometimes		
	written mL)	yard	yd

CHAPTER 2

EXACT MEASURES

This handy reference book is written to give you *easy* ways to measure without doing complicated arithmetic or constantly using a calculator. But there can be everyday occasions when precise measurements are necessary. So *exact* figures are given and explained in this chapter to provide a point of reference when required.

EXACT EQUIVALENT MEASURES OF WEIGHT

Weight denotes how heavy something is, whether it is the weight of nuts in a fruit cake or the weight of a boxer.

It can be seen in the following chart that exact conversions run to several decimal places. As this is often impractical, the numbers are often rounded up or down to just one decimal place, or the nearest whole number is used depending on the accuracy desired. For instance the exact metric equivalent of 1 ounce is 28.3495 grams or it can be rounded to one decimal place which is 28.4 grams or given the nearest whole figure which is 28 grams.

Once figures are rounded up or down they can become very inaccurate especially if they are multiplied, so it is often important to have an exact figure to which to refer, as given in the following lists.

1 ounce equals	28.3495	grams
	0.0625	pounds
	0.028350	kilograms

1 pound equals	16	ounces
	453.592	grams
	0.453592	kilograms
14 pounds (1 stone) equals	6.350	kilograms
28 pounds equals 1 quarter	12.7	kilograms
1 hundredweight (4 quarters) equals	50.8023	kilograms
	112	pounds
	1792	ounces
	50802.3	grams
	0.056	US ton (short ton)
	0.05080	tonne
	0.05	UK ton
1 UK ton equals	1.01605	tonne
	1.12	US ton
	20	hundredweight
	1016.05	kilogram
	2240	pounds
	35840	ounces
1 gram equals	0.035274	ounces
1 kilogram equals	2.20462	pounds
	35.2740	ounces
	0.019684	hundredweight
1 US ton equals	0.907185	tonne
	0.892857	UK ton
	17.8571	hundredweight
	907.185	kilograms
	2000	pounds
	32000	ounces
	907185	grams

1 tonne equals	0.984207	UK tons
	1.10231	US ton
	19.6841	hundredweight
	1000	kilogram
	2204.62	pounds
	35273.9	ounces

EXACT EQUIVALENT MEASURES OF LENGTH, (DISTANCE), BREADTH AND HEIGHT

Whether measuring the width across a cake tin, the depth of an oven, the height of a room when wallpapering or the distance from home to the village hall, the measurements given below are required.

Length is the distance between two points. When measuring a rectangular item such as a loaf tin, the length is always the longer of the two sides.

Distance is also related to length, for instance how far is the bus stop from your house.

Breadth is the term used for the width of something, the measurement across a running track or the shorter of the two sides of a rectangular tin.

Height and **depth** are vertical measures; for instance the distance from the top of a building to the ground or from the top rim of a cake tin to the base.

Small measures are given in inches, millimetres or centimetres.

Larger measures are given in feet, yards, metres or kilometres.

1 inch equals	25.4	millimetres
	2.54	centimetres
	0.0254	metres
	0.083333	feet
	0.027778	yards

1 foot equals	304.8	millimetres
	30.48	centimetres
	0.3048	metre
	12	inches
	0.333333	yards
1 yard equals	914.4	millimetres
	91.44	centimetres
	0.9144	metres
	36	inches
	3	feet
1 centimetre equals	10	millimetres
	0.01	metres
	0.393701	inches
	0.032808	feet
	0.010936	yards
1 metre equals	100	centimetres
	1000	millimetres
	39.3701	inches
	3.28084	feet
	1.09361	yards

Millimetres

1 centimetre can be divided into 10 millimetres
1 metre can be divided into 1,000 millimetres
1 millimetre is equal to 0.0394 inches

To convert inches to exact millimetres -

multiply the number of inches by 25.4 for an exact answer.

To convert inches to exact millimetres and centimetres

Inches	Millimetres	Centimetres
1	25.4	2.54
2	50.8	5.08
3	76.2	7.62
4	101.6	10.16
5	127.0	12.70
6 (half a foot)	152.4	15.24
7	177.8	17.78
8	203.2	20.32
9	228.6	22.86
10	254.0	25.40
20	508.0	50.80
30	762.0	76.20
40	1016.0	101.60
50	1270.0	127.00
60	1524.0	152.40
70	1778.0	177.80
80	2032.0	203.20
90	2286.0	228.60
100	2540.0	254.00

To convert millimetres to exact inches -

multiply the number of millimetres by 0.0394 for an exact answer or multiply by 0.04 for an approximate answer.

When the answer is larger than 10 it is usual to express the answer in centimetres and millimetres rather than a very large number of millimetres.

To convert millimetres and centimetres to inches

Metric mm	Imperial inches	Metric mm	Imperial inches
2	$^1/_{16}$ inch	18	7
3	$^1/_8$	19	7 ½
5	¼	20 cm	8 inches
8	$^3/_8$	22	8 ½
10 mm/1cm	½	23	9
15 mm	$^5/_8$	24	9 ½
2 cm	¾	25 cm	10 inches
2.5 cm	1 inch	26	10 ½
3	1 ¼	27	10 ¾
4	1 ½	28	11
4.5	1 ¾	29	11 ½
5 cm	2 inches	30 cm	12 inches
5.5	2 ¼	31	12 ½
6	2 ½	33	13
7	2 ¾	34	13 ½
7.5	3	35	14
8	3 ¼	37	14 ½
9	3 ½	38	15
9.5	3 ¾	39	15 ½
10 cm	4 inches	40 cm	16 inches
11	4 ¼	42	16 ½
12	4 ½	43	17
13	5	44	17 ½
14	5 ½	46	18
15	6	48	19
16	6 ¼	50 cm	20 inches
17	6 ½		

Centimetres

Centi means one hundreth so -
1 metre can be divided into 100 centimetres written 100 cm
1 centimetre is exactly equal to 0.3937 inches or 0.4 inches when rounded to the nearest inch.

To convert inches to exact centimetres -
multiply the number of inches by 2.54 for an exact
answer or multiply by 2.5 for an approximate answer.

To convert centimetres to exact inches -
multiply the number of centimetres by 0.3937 for an exact answer or multiply by 0.4 for an approximate answer.

To convert feet to exact centimetres -
multiply the number of feet by 30.48 for an exact answer or multiply by 30.5 for an approximate answer.

To convert yards to exact centimetres -
multiply the number of yards by 91.44 for an exact answer or multiply by 91.5 for an approximate answer.

When any answer or figure is more than 100 cm it is usual to express the answer in metres and centimetres rather than a very large number of centimetres.

Metre

The metre can be divided into 100 parts each called a centimetre and can be divided into 1000 parts each called a millimetre.

1 yard is 3 feet or 36 inches

1 metre is just over 1 yard - 39.37 inches

Rounding this figure to the nearest whole number means 1 metre equals 39 inches

To convert feet to exact metres -
multiply the number of feet by 0.3048 for an exact answer or 0.31 for an approximate answer

To convert yards to exact metres -
multiply the number of yards by 0.9144 for an exact answer or 0.9 for an approximate answer.

To convert metres to exact feet -
multiply the number of metres by 3.2808 for an exact answer or 3.3 for an approximate answer.

To convert metres to exact yards -
multiply the number of metres by 1.0936 for an exact answer or 1.1 for an approximate answer.

To convert feet to exact metres -

Feet	Metres
1	0.305
2	0.610
3 (1 yard)	0.914
4	1.219
5	1.524
6 (2 yard)	1.829
7	2.134
8	2.438
9 (3 yard)	2.743
10	3.048

To convert yards to exact metres

Yards	Metres
1 (3 feet)	0.914
2	1.829
3	2.743
4	3.658
5	4.572
6	5.486
7	6.401
8	7.315
9	8.230
10 (30 feet)	9.144

To convert metres to exact feet and yards

Metres	Feet	Yards
1	3.281	1.094
2	6.562	2.187
3	9.843	3.281
4	13.123	4.374
5	16.404	5.468
6	19.685	6.562
7	22.966	7.655
8	26.247	8.749
9	29.528	9.843
10	32.808	10.936

1 mile or 1,760 yards or 5,280 feet equals 1.60993 kilometres

1 British Nautical Mile equals 2026.66 yards or 6.080 feet or 1.15 statute miles

EXACT EQUIVALENT MEASURES OF VOLUME

Volume is the term used to measure amounts of liquid whether the amount of milk to be added in a recipe or the amount of petrol put in a car.

Small amounts are usually described in millilitres while large amounts are always measured in litres.

Millilitre

1 litre can be divided into millilitres
Milli means one thousand so there are one thousand millilitres in 1 litre and therefore five hundred millilitres in ½ litre.

Centilitre
1 litre can be divided into centilitres
Centi means one hundred so there are 100 centilitres in 1 litre.

Decilitre
The litre can be divided into decilitres
Deci means 10 so there are 10 decilitres in 1 litre.

10 millilitres (ml)	=	1 centilitre	(cl)
10 centilitres (cl)	=	1 decilitre	(dl)
10 decilitres (dl)	=	1 litre	(l)
10 litres (l)	=	1 decalitre	(dal)
10 decalitres (dal)	=	1 hectolitre	(hl)
10 hectolitres(hl)	=	1 kilolitre	(kl)

To convert fluid ounces and pints to millilitres and litres
The rounded off measurement, while not necessarily the nearest whole number is the one used in recipes in the UK

Imperial Measure	Exact ml figure	Rounded off ml measure
1 fl.oz	28.413	25
2	56.826	50
3	85.239	85
4	113.652	100
5 fl.oz (¼ pint)	142.065	150
6	170.478	170
7 fl.oz (¹/₃ pint)	198.891	200
8	227.305	225
9	255.718	250
10 fl.oz (½ pint)	284.131	300
15 fl.oz (¾ pint)	426.196	425
20 fl.oz (1 pint)	568.261	575
25 fl.oz (1¼ pint)	710.326	700
30 fl.oz (1½ pint)	852.392	850
35 fl.oz (1¾ pint)	994.457	1 litre
2 pints	1136.523	1.1
2¼	1278.588	1.3
2½	1420.654	1.4
2¾	1562.719	1.6
3	1704.784	1.7
3¼	1846.849	1.8
3½	1988.915	2.0
3¾	2130.98	2.1
4	2273.046	2.3
4¼		2.4
4½	2557.177	2.6
4¾		2.7
5	2841.307	2.8
5¼ pints		3.0 litre
5½		3.1 litre
5¾		3.3 litre

Imperial Measure	Exact ml figure	Rounded off ml measure
6	3409.568	3.4 litre
6¼		3.5 litre
6½		3.7 litre
6¾		3.8 litre
7	3977.83	4.0 litre
8 pints (1 gallon)	4546.092	4.5 litre
9	5114.353	5.1 litre
10 pints	5682.614	5.7 litre

To convert millilitres to fluid ounces

ml		fl oz
1	=	0.035
2		0.070
3		0.106
4		0.141
5		0.176
6		0.211
7		0.246
8		0.282
9		0.317
10		0.352
20		0.704
28.413 ml	=	1 fluid ounce
30 ml	=	1.056 fl oz

The exact conversion figures given below have many decimal points and as with the other measurements are usually rounded off to the nearest 0.5 or 5.

1 fluid ounce	equals	28.41	millilitres
1 UK pint		568.2	millilitres
1 UK gallon		1.201	US gallons
		4.546	litres
		4546	millilitres
1 US gallon	equals	3.785	litres
		3785	millilitres
		0.8327	UK gallons
1 litre	equals	1000	millilitres
		0.2642	US gallons
		0.2200	UK gallons
1 litre	equals	1.760	UK pints
1 US barrel	equals	42	US gallons = 34.97 UK gallons

Not often found now but common in old recipes is the use of the gill and the quart.

1 gill   =   0.1421 litres
4 gills   = 1 pint =0.5683 litres
2 pints = 1 quart = 1.1366 litres
4 quarts = 1 gallon = 4.4561 litres
1 peck   = 2 gallons
8 gallons (4 pecks) = 1 bushel
8 bushels = 1 quater

EXACT EQUIVALENT MEASURES OF AREA

An area is always called 'square', a square foot, a square metre and so on. The little '2' above the measure symbol means 'squared'. Use square metres for small areas such as an area of a room. Use square kilometres for large areas such as the area of a park. Use hectares for large areas of land such as fields and farms. When measuring any large area it is wise to use the exact figures below and then round off the answer to get a more precise final figure.

1 inch²	equals	645.16	millimetres²
		6.4516	centimetres²
1 foot²	equals	144	inches²
		0.1111	yards²
		929	centimetres²
		92903	millimetres²
		0.09290	metres²
1 yard²	equals	9	feet²
		1296	inches²
		8361	centimetres²
		836127	millimetres²
		0.8361	metres²
1 cm²	equals	100	millimetres²
		0.1550	inches²
1 metre²	equals	1.196	yard²
		10.764	feet²
		1550	inches²
		10,000	centimetres²

Written another way - in words -

1 square foot	equals	144	square inches
1 square yard		9	square feet

To convert square metres to square feet

square metre		square feet	square metre		square feet
1	equals	10.764	20	equals	215.278
2		21.528	30		322.917
3		32.292	40		430.556
4		43.056	50		538.196
5		53.820	60		645.835
6		64.583	70		753.474
7		75.347	80		861.113
8		86.111	90		968.752
9		96.875	100		1076.391
10		107.639			

To change square feet to square yards divide by 9 as there are 9 square feet in 1 square yard.

To convert square feet to square metres

square feet		square metre	square feet		square metre
1	equals	0.093	20	equals	1.858
2		0.186	30		2.787
3		0.279	40		3.716
4		0.372	50		4.645
5		0.465	60		5.574
6		0.557	70		6.503
7		0.650	80		7.432
8		0.743	90		8.361
9		0.836	100		9.290
10		0.929			

MEASURING THE AREA OF VARIOUS SHAPES

These formulae enable measurements of circular and spherical objects to be calculated.

$\pi = 22 \div 7$ or 3.14

To find the -

circumference of a circle use the formulae	$2\pi r$
area of a circle	πr^2
volume of a sphere	πr^3
surface of a sphere	$4\pi r^2$
volume of a cylinder	$\pi r^2 h$

MEASUREMENT OF LAND AREA

1 acre $= 4047$ m^2
1 acre $= 4840$ square yards
1 kilometre^2 $= 100$ hectare or 247.1 acre
1 mile^2 $= 2.590$ kilometre^2 or 259.0 hectare or 640 acres

Equivalent measures are taken to the nearest 0.001

To convert acres to hectares

acres		hectares	acres		hectares
1	=	0.405	8	=	3.237
2		0.809	9		3.642
3		1.214	10		4.047
4		1.619	20		8.094
5		2.023	30		12.140
6		2.428	40		16.187
7		2.833	50		20.234

To convert hectares to acres

hectares		acres		hectares		acres
1	=	2.471		8	=	19.769
2		4.942		9		22.240
3		7.413		10		24.711
4		9.884		20		49.421
5		12.355		30		74.132
6		14.826		40		98.842
7		17.297		50		123.553

1 acre equals	4047	metres²
	4840	yards²
	43,560	feet²
	0.4047	hectare
1 hectare equals	2.471	acres
	10,000	metres²
	11,960	yards²
	107,639	feet²

EXACT EQUIVALENT MEASUREMENTS OF TEMPERATURE

Temperature is measured in degrees. These may be degrees Fahrenheit (F) or degrees Celsius (C), both named after the gentlemen who introduced them.

Degrees F may still be found on some very old kitchen cookers and often in many old recipes.

Degrees C should now be used in the kitchen, for weather forecasting and when measuring the temperature of the body. The Centigrade scale is often called this because it is divided into 100 equal divisions. Its correct name is the Celsius scale named after the Swedish astronomer and physicist Anders Celsius (1701 - 1744).

Everyone should now use degrees C but what is important is that the two types of measure are not mixed in the same context. Some thermometers are marked in Celsius (centigrade) *and* Fahrenheit scales.

This section shows the equivalent temperatures to enable you to convert quickly from one to the other if necessary but it is much better and safer if you get used to using Celsius all the time.

Centigrade		Fahrenheit	Centigrade		Fahrenheit
0° C	is the same as	32° F	36° C	is the same as	97° F
5°		41°	37°		99°
10°		50°	38°		100°
15°		59°	39°		102°
20°		68°	40°		104°
21°		70°	45°		113°
22°		72°	50°		122°
23°		73°	55°		131°
24°		75°	60°		140°
25°		77°	70°		158°
26°		79°	80°		176°
27°		80°	90°		194°
28°		82°	100°		212°
29°		84°			
30°		86°			
31°		88°			
32°		90°			
33°		92°			
34°		93°			
35°		95°			

COMPARATIVE TEMPERATURES

To avoid having to look up equivalent temperatures on a chart, or when a chart is not available, there is a quick way to convert from one temperature scale to the other but it is far easier to get used to using the Celsius scale.

To change Celsius to Fahrenheit -
multiply the Celsius figure by 9, divide that answer by 5 and add 32. The answer is ° Fahrenheit.
Put as an equation °F = 9/5 (°C + 32)

To change Fahrenheit to Celsius -
subtract 32 from the Fahrenheit figure, multiply by 5 and divide this figure by 9. The answer is ° Celsius.
Put as an equation °C = 5/9 (°F - 32)

Commonly used temperatures
The boiling point of water is   100°C or 212°F
The freezing point of water is   0°C or 32°F
Temperatures below freezing   - 0°C have a minus sign in front

(For oven temperatures see page 115)

SOME OF THE MEASURES GIVEN BELOW ARE RARELY USED IN EVERYDAY SITUATIONS NOW BUT CAN BE VERY HELPFUL AND INTERESTING TO REFER TO ON SOME OCCASIONS

1,000	micrometres	equal	1	millimetre
10	millimetres		1	centimetre
10	centimetres		1	decimetre
10	decimetres		1	metre
10	metres		1	decametre
10	decametres		1	hectometre
10	hectometres		1	kilometre

1,000	microgrammes	equal	1	milligramme
10	milligrammes		1	centigramme
10	centigrammes		1	decigramme
10	decigrammes		1	gramme
10	grammes		1	decagramme
10	decagrammes		1	hectogramme
10	hectogrammes		1	kilogramme
1,000	kilogrammes		1	tonne

10	millilitres	equal	1	centilitre
10	centilitres		1	decilitre
10	decilitres		1	litre
10	litres		1	decalitre
10	decalitres		1	hectolitre
10	hectolitres		1	kilolitre
4	gills		1	pint
2	pints		1	quart
4	quarts		1	gallon
2	gallons		1	peck
8	gallons		4	pecks = 1 bushel
8	bushels		1	quarter

1	acre	equals	4 roods = 4840 square yards
1	rood		¼ acre = 1210 square yards = 40 square poles
1	decre		10 acres
1	hectare		100 acres
1	rod, pole or perch		16½ feet = 25 links
1	pole		25 links
1	chain		100 links = 22 yards = 66 feet or 4 poles
4	pecks		1 bushel = 8 gallons

1	furlong		40	rods
			220	yards
			10	chains
1	mile		8	furlongs
			or 1760	yards
			or 5280	feet
			or 80	= chains = 1760 yards
1	square mile		640	acres
1	league		3	miles
1	link		7.92	inches
1	fathom	equals	6	feet
1	league		3	nautical miles
1	British Nautical Mile		6080	feet
			or 2026.66	yards
			or 1.15	statute miles
1	knot		1 British Nautical Mile per hour	

MONEY

Pre-decimal currency which was introduced in February 1971

1 penny (d)	=	4 farthings
	=	2 half pennies
12 pence	=	1 shilling (s)
5 shillings	=	1 crown
2 shillings and six pence	=	half a crown
4 crowns = 2 shillings	=	1 pound (£1.00)
21 shillings	=	1 guinea

CHAPTER 3

WEIGHTS AND MEASURES
FOR COOKS IN A UK KITCHEN

If you have a recipe giving weights of ingredients in Imperial measures and you have Imperial scales and jugs then you can follow that recipe with confidence. If you have a recipe which only gives ingredients in metric quantities and you have metric scales and measuring jugs then measuring is easy. If cup sizes are given they may be UK, USA or Australian cups. Check to make sure you have the correct standard cups, otherwise use the conversion charts in this chapter which enable you to change from one way of measuring to the other as necessary.

In 1969 it was decided that in the United Kingdom kitchen one ounce should be taken as being the equivalent of 25 grams and this is the calculation still used in Britain today. No other equivalents are fixed, they differ according to the recipe. For instance in some recipes 4 ounces is taken to be 100 grams while in others it appears as 115 grams.

The calculation below shows how this figure is arrived at.

In the first chapter on 'Exact Equivalent Measures' it can be seen that the exact equivalent of 1 ounce is 28.3495 grams.

Therefore 2 ounce is equivalent to 56.6990 grams, or rounded off, 57 grams. If 2 ounces is written in a recipe as 50 grams, an easy nice round figure, the fact that the ingredient will weigh 7 gram less than it would be in exact Imperial measures is unlikely to matter much in many recipes.

However when 4 ounces is required, the exact equivalent is 4 x 28.3495 which equals 113.3980 g. This is quite a long way from calling 4 ounces 100 grams so it is often rounded up to 115 grams, i.e. the nearest five grams.

It really all depends on whether you are making something like a casserole where exact weights of ingredients don't matter much, or a cake where exact measures can be vital for success.

TO CONVERT IMPERIAL MEASURES TO METRIC MEASURES IN RECIPES

To convert from an Imperial to metric measure or metric to Imperial measure, look up the amount to be changed in the first column and read off the amount alongside in the next column. This chart gives the exact whole number of grams in ounces up to one pound with the gram conversion to the nearest 25g in the third column.

Imperial ounce	Gram conversion to nearest round figure	Recommended gram conversion to nearest 25 gram figure
$^1/_8$	5	
$^1/_4$	10	
$^1/_2$	15	
$^3/_4$	20	
1	28	25
2	57	50
3	85	75
4 ($^1/_4$ lb)	113	100-125
5	142	150
6	170	175
7	198	200
8 ($^1/_2$ lb)	227	225
9	255	250
10	284	300
11	311	325
12 ($^3/_4$ lb)	340	350
13	368	375
14	396	400
15	425	425
16 (1 lb)	453	450

Imperial ounce	Gram conversion to nearest round figure	Recommended gram conversion to nearest 25 gram figure
1 ¼ pound	550	
1 ½	675	
2 ¼	900 grams	1 kilogram
2 ½	1 ¼	
3	1 ½	
3 ½	1 ¾	
4	1 ¾	
4 ½	2	
5 pound	2 ¼ kilogram	

TO CONVERT OUNCES AND POUNDS TO THE NEAREST 5 GRAMS AND KILOGRAMS

Where no amount is given, obtain the total by adding two numbers together.

For instance if the recipe states that 7½ ounces are needed, in grams this would be 198 + 14 = 212 grams or nearest 210 g

TO CONVERT GRAMS AND KILOGRAMS TO OUNCES AND POUNDS

grams	ounces		grams	ounces
5	¹⁄₈		75	2¾
10	¼		85	5
15	½		90	3¼
20	¾		100	3½
25	4		115	6
35	1¼		125	4½
40	1½		140	7
50	1¾		150	5½
55	5		175	6
60	2¼		200	7
70	2½			

grams	pound	ounces		grams	pound	ounces
225		8		500	1	2
250		9		550	1	4
275		9½		600	1	5
280		11		650	1	7
300		10½		700	1	9
325		11½		750	1	10
350		12		800	1	12
375		13		850	1	14
400		14		900	2	
425		15		950	2	2
450		1				

kilograms	pound	ounces
1	2	4
1.25	2	12
1.3	3	
1.5	3	5
1.6	3	8
1.8	4	
2	4	8
2.25	5	
2.5	5	8
2.7	6	
3	6	8

TO CONVERT FLUID OUNCES AND PINTS TO MILLILITRES AND LITRES

Imperial measure	Metric measure	Imperial measure	Metric measure
1 fluid ounce	25 ml	20 fluid (1 UK pint) exact measure 568 often taken as	600
2	50		
3	75		
4	125	1½	850
5	150	1¾	1 litres
6	175	2	1¼
7	200	2½	1½
8	225	3	1¾
9	250	3½	2
10 (half pint)	300	4	2¼
12	350	4½	2½
14	400	5	2¾
16	450	6	3½
18	500	7	4
		8 pints (1 gallon)	4½

TO CONVERT MILLILITRES AND LITRES TO FLUID OUNCES, PINTS AND USA CUPS

Millilitres		Fluid Ounces	American Cups
25	equals	1	
50		2	
65		2½	
85		3	
100		3½	

Millilitres	Fluid Ounces	American Cups
120	4	
135	4½	
150	5 (¼ pint)	
175	6	
200	7 (¹/₃ pint)	
250	8 equals	1
275	9	
300	10 (½ pint)	
350	12	
400	14	
450	15 (¾ pint)	
475	16 equals	2
500	18	
600	20 (1UK pint)	
750	1¼ Pints	
790	1½	
1 litres	1¾	
1.2	2	
1.5	2½	
1.75	3	
2	3½	
2.25	4	
2.5	4½	
2.75	5	
4.55	8 (1 UK gallon)	

EXACT EQUIVALENT QUANTITIES TO THE UK PINT

1 pint = 20 fluid ounces = 568 millilitres
¾ pint = 15 fluid ounces = 326 millilitres
½ pint = 10 fluid ounces = 284 millilitres
¼ pint = 5 fluid ounces = 142 millilitres

0.88 pints = ½ litre
1.76 pints - just over 1¾ pints = 1 litre
8 pints = 1 gallon which is just over 4½ litres
1 litre = 1.76 pints - a little more than 1¾ pints
½ litre = 0.88 pints
4½ litres = just under 1 gallon
1 litre = 4½ American cups

There are 568 millilitres in 1 Imperial pint but it is very common to find the 1 pint equivalent given in a recipe as either 550 ml or 600 ml where the exact amount of liquid used is not too important, for instance the amount of stock added to a stew.

WEIGHING DRY INGREDIENTS

The weights of dry ingredients in a recipe are usually given in grams or ounces. Yet it can often be quicker, more convenient and you don't have to wash a scale pan if you measure in tablespoons. It is also surprising how few people have scales of any kind.

All tablespoon measures given below are *level* tablespoons as these are more accurate. It must be remembered that this method of measuring is accurate enough for most recipes but the amounts are likely to vary a little according to whether the food is packed into the spoon or it is just lightly filled.

To use this method of measuring it is important to use **exact standard** UK measuring spoons which can be bought from kitchen shops, department stores and some supermarkets. Do not use a tablespoon from a canteen of cutlery as they are not a standard measure or size.

TABLESPOON EQUIVALENTS TO 25 GRAMS/1 OUNCE OF COMMONLY USED FOODS

3 tablespoons	breadcrumbs - dried
6 tablespoons	breadcrumbs - fresh
1½ tablespoons	brown sugar
2 tablespoons	butter or margarine
2 tablespoons	caster, granulated sugar
4 tablespoons	cheese - grated, hard variety
3 tablespoons	cocoa powder
3½ tablespoons	curry powder
5 tablespoons	desiccated coconut
2 tablespoons	dried fruits, raisins, sultanas and currants
1½ tablespoons	dried yeast
3½ tablespoons	dry mustard
2½ tablespoons	flour, custard powder or cornflour
2 tablespoons	gelatine powder
1 tablespoon	golden syrup
1 tablespoon	grated chocolate
4 tablespoons	ground almonds, hazelnuts, walnuts and mixed nuts
4 tablespoons	ground coffee
3 tablespoons	ground ginger
2½ tablespoons	icing sugar
6 tablespoons	instant coffee powder
4 tablespoons	porridge oats
1½ tablespoons	rice - uncooked
1 tablespoon	salt
3 tablespoons	semolina
1 tablespoon	syrup, honey, treacle and jam

CHAPTER 4

WEIGHTS AND MEASURES IN THE AMERICAN KITCHEN

There are many American cookery books on sale in Britain and Europe. There are also many British cookery books on sale in America. It is a great pity that due to the difficulties in understanding equivalent measurements, many of these recipes are not attempted by those who would like to cook them.

The American cup system of measuring is still the most widely used in the USA, but if ingredients are weighed, most American cooks usually weigh in Imperial measures. For those living in Britain who wish to use cups as printed in an American recipe, standard USA cups can be bought from good kitchen shops and large department stores in Britain. Make sure they are standard USA cups and not British cups which are different. If you want to cook an American recipe and have no standard USA cups, then use the charts in this section to convert the cup quantities listed in the recipe into Imperial or metric measures whichever you prefer.

If an American cook wishes to cook recipes that are written in metric or Imperial measures with which she is unfamiliar, then using the information given here the quantities of ingredients listed can be converted into cups from metric or Imperial measures.

It is important to note that measurement conversion is an inexact science and great care is needed in switching figures if a special recipe needing exact proportions is being cooked.

METRIC, IMPERIAL AND AMERICAN CUP EQUIVALENT MEASURES

If the food you are wishing to include in a recipe does not appear in this list then choose a food which is very similar and use that conversion figure.

	Imperial	Metric	American Cups	Tablespoons
Almonds-whole blanched	4 oz	100 g	3/4	
-ground	2½ oz	65 g	1/2	
Bacon - diced raw	2 oz	50 g	1/3	
Breadcrumbs - fresh	2 oz	50 g	1	
- dried	2 oz	50 g	3/4	
Butter, Margarine and White Fats	½ oz	15 g		1
(pack tightly into cup)	3/4 oz	20 g		1½
	1 oz	25 g		2
	1½ oz	42 g		3
	2 oz	50 g		4
	2½ oz	65 g		5
	3 oz	85 g		6
	4 oz	100 g	½ = 1 stick	8
	5 oz	125 g	5/8	
	6 oz	150 g	3/4	
	8 oz	225 g	1	
Cereals				
pearl barley/ tapioca	4 oz	100 g	1/2	
corn meal	6 oz	150 g	1	
cracked wheat	6 oz	150 g	1	
semolina/ground rice	6 oz	150 g	1	
oatmeal	3 oz	75 g	1	
Cheese				
grated hard	½ oz	15 g		2
	1 oz	25 g	1/4	

	Imperial	Metric	American Cups	Tablespoons
	2 oz	50 g	$^1/_2$	
	4 oz	100 g	1	
Parmesan	1 oz	25 g		3
	2 oz	50 g	$^1/_3$	
	4 oz	100 g	$^2/_3$	
cottage cheese	2 oz	50 g	$^1/_3$	
	4 oz	100 g	$^2/_3$	
	6 oz	150 g	1	
Cornflour/Cornstarch				
	$^1/_2$ oz	15 g		$1^1/_2$
	1 oz	25 g		3
	2 oz	50 g		6
	4 oz	100 g	$^3/_4$	
Cream				
	2 fl oz	56 ml	$^1/_4$	4
	3 fl oz	85 ml		6
	4 fl oz	115 ml	$^1/_2$	
	5 fl oz ($^1/_4$ pint)	142 ml	$^5/_8$	
	$^1/_2$ pint	284 ml	$1^1/_4$	
	1 pint	568 ml	$2^1/_2$	
sour -cream	5 oz carton	142 ml	1	
curry powder	$^1/_2$ oz	15 g		1
	1 oz	25 g		2
Dried fruit				
currants, raisins	1 oz	25 g		2
	2 oz	50 g	$^1/_3$ cup packed	
	4 oz	100 g	$^2/_3$ cup packed	
	6 oz	150 g	1 cup packed	

	Imperial	Metric	American Cups	Tablespoons
prunes	2 oz	50 g	$3/8$	
	6 oz	150 g	1 generous cup	
dried apricots	2 oz	50 g	$3/8$	
	4 oz	100 g	$3/4$	
	6 oz	150 g	1 generous cup	
	8 oz	225 g	$1\frac{1}{2}$	
candied peel	2 oz	50 g	$\frac{1}{2}$	
	4 oz	100 g	1	
glace cherries	4 oz	100 g	bare $\frac{1}{2}$ cup	
	8 oz	225 g	good $\frac{1}{2}$ cup	
apple rings	2 oz	50 g	$1\frac{1}{2}$ cups	
	4 oz	100 g	$2\,2/3$	

EGGS

approximate weights

very large	73 g and over
large	63-73 g
medium	53-63 g
small	53 g and under

American egg measures

approximate measures

	American Cups	Tablespoons
1 egg white		$1\frac{1}{2}$
1 egg yolk		1
12 - 14 egg yolks	1	
8-10 egg whites	1	
4 -6 eggs	1	
4 egg whites	$\frac{1}{2}$	

Flour

plain/all purpose (sifted before being measured and not packed tight in the cup)

	Imperial	Metric	American Cups	Tablespoons
	$\frac{1}{2}$ oz	15 g		2
	1 oz	25 g		4

	Imperial	Metric	American Cups	Tablespoons
	2 oz	50 g	good ½ cup	
	3 oz	75 g	good ¾ cup	
	3½ oz	90 g	1	
	4 oz	100 g	1 cup + 2 tbs	
	8 oz	225 g	2¼	
	16 oz (1 pound)	450 g	4½	
Gelatine	½ oz	15 g		2
	1 oz	25 g	¼	4
Honey, jam, syrup	4 oz	100 g	$3/8$	
	6 oz	150 g	½	
	8 oz	225 g	¾	
	12 oz	340 g	1	
	16 oz (1 pound)	450 g	1 $3/8$	
Ice Cream	6 oz	150 g	½	
	8 oz	225 g	1	
Pasta	8 oz	225 g	1 $2/3$	
MEAT				
diced cooked meat	3 oz	75 g	½	
	6 oz	150 g	1	
	8 oz	225 g	1 $1/3$	
minced (ground) meat	4 oz	100 g	½	
	8 oz	225 g	1	
	12 oz	340 g	1½	
	16 oz (1 pound)	450 g	2	
NUTS				
walnuts shelled	2 oz	50 g	½ generous cup	
shelled	4 oz	100 g	1 generous cup	

	Imperial	Metric	American Cups	Tablespoons
ground nuts	2 oz	50 g	½	
	4 oz	100 g	1	
small nuts - see almonds				
Olives	2½ oz	70 g	½	
	4 oz	100 g	1	
PULSES				
haricot beans	6 oz	150 g	1	
kidney beans	11 oz	310 g	1	
lentils	6 oz	150 g	1	
RICE				
long grain	2 oz	50 g	¼	
	4 oz	100 g	½	
	8 oz	225 g	1 good cup	
Note 1 cup of raw rice yields	approx. 3 cups cooked rice			
short grain	2 oz	50 g	¼	
	4 oz	100 g	½	
	8 oz	225 g	1	
SUGAR				
caster/granulated	1 oz	25 g		1
	2 oz	50 g	¼	
	3 oz	75 g	¹/₃	
	4 oz	100 g	½	
	5 oz	140 g	²/₃	
	6 oz	170 g	¾	
	7 oz	198 g	bare 1 cup	
	8 oz	225 g	1	
icing/confectioners sugar (sifted)				
	1 oz	25 g	¼	
	2 oz	50 g	bare ½ cup	
	3 oz	75 g	²/₃	
	4 oz	100 g	¾	

	Imperial	Metric	American Cups	Tablespoons
	5 oz	140 g	bare cup	
	6 oz	170 g	1	
	7 oz	198 g	1 $^1/_3$	
	8 oz	225 g	1 $^2/_3$	
	12 oz	340 g	2½	
	16 oz (1 pound)	450 g	3 $^1/_3$	
soft brown/dark brown (firmly packed)				
	1 oz	25 g		2
	2 oz	50 g	¼	
	3 oz	75 g	$^1/_3$	
	4 oz	100 g	½	
	6 oz	170 g	¾	
	8 oz	225 g	1	
	12 oz	340 g	1½	
	16 oz (1 pound)	450 g	2	
Shrimps shelled	4 oz	100 g	¾	
shelled	8 oz	225 g	1½	
Tomato puree concentrate				
	¾ oz	20 g		1½
	2¼ oz	60 g		3
	3 oz	75 g		6
	3¾ oz	85 g		7½
	4½ oz	115 g		9
	9 oz	255 g		18

In order to enjoy success with all recipes it is necessary to understand the cookery terms used for foods and equipment in other countries. Imagining what the terms mean can cause a disaster, so 'translations' of these are given below.

BRITISH / AMERICAN TERMINOLOGY FOR FOODS

British	American
ale	light ale or beer
almonds - ground	almonds - finely ground
almonds - flaked	slivered almonds
anchovy essence	anchovy paste
apples - cooking	green apples
apple pips	apple seeds
aubergine	egg plant
avocado stone	avocado seed
bacon joint	baked ham
baking powder	baking powder
beans - french or green	snap beans
beans - haricot	white beans
beetroot	beet
beef olives	roulades
beef stock cubes	beef bouillon cube
bicarbonate of soda	baking soda
bilberries	blueberries
biscuits	cookies
biscuit mixture	cookie dough
bread rusks	zwieback crackers
broad beans	windsor or fava beans

British	American
butter beans	lima beans
butter - unsalted	sweet butter
cake mixture	cake batter
cauliflower sprigs	cauliflowerets
cherries cooking	cherries tart or sour
cherry stones	cherry pits
chick peas	garbanzo beans
chicken joint	chicken quarter
chicory	Belgian endive
chocolate - plain	semi-sweet chocolate pieces
chocolate - cooking	unsweetened chocolate
cider	apple cider
coconut - dessicated	coconut - flaked or grated or shredded
coriander - fresh	cilantro
cornflour	corn starch
cos lettuce	romaine
courgettes	zucchini
crayfish	crawfish
cream crackers	oyster crackers
cream - double	heavy cream or whipping cream
- single	light cream
crystallised fruits	candied fruits
cucumber pickles	dill pickles
custard powder	no equivalent use cornstarch + yellow colouring
curd cheese	farmer's cheese
curly endive	chicory

British	American
dairy produce	dairy products
dates - stoned	dates - pitted
demerara sugar	light brown sugar
desiccated coconut	shredded coconut
digestive biscuits	Graham crackers
drop scone	pancake
egg - hard boiled	egg - hard cooked
endive	chicory
entrecote steak	Porterhouse steak
fats e.g. lard	shortening
flaked almonds	sliced almonds
flan	pie crust or pastry shell
flour - plain	all purpose flour
flour - self raising	self rising flour
french beans	snap beans
fresh	raw
full fat cheese	cream cheese
gelatine	gelatin
ginger nuts	ginger snaps
glace cherries	candied cherries
golden syrup	none-use corn syrup -light or dark
ham - parma	prosciutto
haricot beans	navy beans
hazel nuts	cob nuts or filberts
icing	frosting

British	American
icing sugar	confectioners sugar
jam	jelly or preserves
jelly	jello
jelly cubes	jelly crystals
joint of meat	roast
ketchup	catsup
maize - flour	cornmeal
- groats	hominy grits
mangetout	snow peas
marrow	large zucchini or summer squash
minced beef	ground beef
muesli	granola
mustard - French	prepared mustard
oatmeal	rolled oats
oil - groundnut	peanut
offal	variety meats
omelette	omelet
onion - Spanish	Spanish or Bermuda onion
onion - spring	scallion or green onion
onion - button	pearl onion
orange and lemon pips	orange and lemon seeds
pancake	crêpe
peach stone	peach pit
persimmons	sharon fruit

British	American
pig's trotters	pig's shanks
plain chocolate	semi-sweet chocolate
plain flour	all-purpose flour
pork fillet	pork tenderloin
porridge oats	rolled oats
potatoes - creamed	potatoes – mashed
prawns	shrimps
prune stone	prune pit
puddings	desserts
rice - round grain or Carolina rice	short-grain rice
runner beans	green beans
salty biscuits	soda crackers
scones	biscuits
semi-skimmed milk	part skim milk
semolina	semolina flour not widely available - use farina
single cream	light cream
soured cream	sour cream
soya beans	soy beans
soya sauce	soy sauce
sponge fingers	ladyfingers
spring greens	spring cabbage
spring onions	scallions
stalk - apples, cherries etc.	stem
starter	appetizer
starters	hors d'oeuvres

British	American
sticks - celery	stalks
streaky bacon rashers	bacon slices
stock	broth
stoned olives	pitted olives
sugar - caster or granulated	granulated
- soft brown	light brown
- demerara	light brown
- cube sugar	sugar cubes
- icing	confectioners
suet	chopped beef suet
sultanas	seedless white or golden raisins
swede	turnip or rutabaga
sweetcorn	corn
swiss roll	jelly roll
tomato ketchup	catsup
tomato puree - concentrate	tomato paste
treacle	molasses
trifle sponge	jelly roll
tunny fish	tuna fish
vanilla essence	vanilla extract
vanilla pod	vanilla bean
vermicelli	fettucine
walnuts	english walnuts
wholemeal	wholewheat
yogurt - natural	plain yogurt

BRITISH / AMERICAN TERMINOLOGY FOR COOKING EQUIPMENT

British	American
baking tray	cookie sheet
butter muslin	cheese cloth
cake tin	baking pan
fork prongs	fork tines
frying pan	skillet
girdle	griddle
greaseproof paper	waxed paper
grill pan	broiler tray
kitchen paper	paper towel
mincer	grinder
mould	mold
palette knife	spatula
pan	tin
pastry case	pie shell
piping bag	decorators bag
pudding basin	oven-proof bowl
ring mould	tube pan
sandwich tin	layer cake pan
sieve	strainer
swiss roll tin	jelly roll pan
tartlet tin	muffin pan
tin	can
whisk	beater

BRITISH / AMERICAN TERMINOLOGY IN COOKING

British	American
biscuit mixture	cookie dough
bottling	canning
cake mixture	cake batter
chop finely	to mince
first course	appetisers
flan	1 crust pie or pastry shell
fresh	raw
to grill	to broil
jelly cubes	jelly crystals
icing	frosting
omelette	omelette
pinch of	dash of
macerate	steep
made-up dishes	prepared dishes
to mince	to grind
mincer	grinder
mould	mold
puddings	desserts
scones	biscuits
tin	can
trifle sponge	jelly roll
to whisk or whip	to beat

METRIC, IMPERIAL AND USA CUP EQUIVALENT MEASURES FOR FRESH FRUIT AND VEGETABLES

Imperial	Metric	American cups
Apples		
1 pound eating peeled & sliced	454 g	$2\,^2/_3$
1 pound cooking - peeled and sliced	454 g	3 medium sized
1 pound eating	454 g	4 medium sized
Asparagus		
1 pound - fresh	454 g	12 -14 spears
Cabbage		
8 oz - sliced	225 g	3 cups - pressed down
Carrots		
1 pound- sliced	454 g	$3\frac{1}{2}$ - 4 cups
Celery		
2 sliced celery stalks		$^3/_4$ - 1 cup
Courgettes		
1 pound	454 g	4 large
Mushrooms		
8 oz fresh sliced	225 g	$2\frac{1}{2}$
8 oz fresh diced	225 g	2
Onions		
8 oz - sliced	225 g	2
1 pound - sliced	454 g	4
8 oz - chopped	225 g	1
Peas		
10 pack frozen	283 g	$2\frac{1}{2}$
Peppers		
1 large - diced		$^3/_4$ - 1

Imperial	Metric	American cups
Potatoes		
1 pound - sliced	450 g	approx 3 cups
1 pound - diced	450g	approx 4
Pulses		
haricot beans		
6 oz	150 g	1
kidney beans		
11 oz	310 g	1
lentils		
6 oz	150 g	1

Soft fruits are sold in America as pints or quarts – 4 cups = 1 quart

Imperial	Metric	American cups
Blackcurrants		
4 oz	100 g	1
Raspberries		
5 oz	140 g	1
Redcurrants		
4 oz	100 g	1
Strawberries		
6 oz	170 g	1
Spinach		
1 pound cooked	454 g	1
Tomato		
1 pound fresh -	454 g	1½ (pulp)
peeled, seeded		
and chopped		
Turnips		
1 pound - peeled and	454 g	2½
quartered		
Watercress		
1 bunch		1½

QUANTITIES OF FOOD EQUIVALENT TO 1 AMERICAN CUP MEASURE

Each of the quantities listed below is the **approximate equivalent** to 1 American cup

e.g. 1 cup of peeled and sliced cooking apples = 100 g or 4 oz
1 cup of dried and chopped apricots   = 175 g or 6 oz

All figures have been rounded off to the nearest 5 g

Food	Metric	Imperial
Apples cooking		
peeled and sliced	100 g	4 oz
Apricots		
dried and chopped	175 g	6 oz
Banana - mashed	225 g	8 oz
- sliced	175 g	6 oz
Beans - dried	175 g	6 oz
Biscuit crumbs e.g.digestives	100 g	4 oz
Breadcrumbs - dried	140 g	4½ oz
Breadcrumbs - fresh	50 g	2 oz
Bran	50 g	2 oz
Butter	225 g	8 oz
Cabbage - raw - shredded	100 g	4 oz
Carrot - raw - sliced	150 g	5 oz
Cheese - cottage	225 g	8 oz
- Cheddar, grated	100 g	4 oz
- cream, curd	225 g	8 oz
- Parmesan, grated	100 g	4 oz
Cherries - whole, glâcé	200 g	7 oz
Cocoa powder	100 g	4 oz

Food	Metric	Imperial
Coconut - desiccated	90 g	3½ oz
Cornflour	140 g	4½ oz
Cornflakes	25 g	1 oz
Cranberries	100 g	4 oz
Cream - single and double	225 ml	8 fl.oz
Currants - dried	150 g	5 oz
Dates		
- whole, dried, stoned	175 g	6 oz
Figs - dried	175 g	6 oz
Flour - plain and self raising	150 g	5 oz
- wholewheat	165 g	5½oz
Honey	350 g	12 oz
Jam	350 g	12 oz
Lard or dripping	225 g	8 oz
Lentils	200 g	7 oz
Macaroni - raw	100 g	4 oz
Marmalade	300 g	11 oz
Mayonnaise	225 g	8 oz
Milk - fresh	225 ml	8 fl.oz
- evaporated	250 ml	9 fl.oz
- condensed	300 ml	11 fl.oz
Milk - powdered - low fat	90 g	3½ oz
Mincemeat	300 g	11 oz
Mixed peel	175 g	6 oz
Mushrooms		
fresh sliced	50 g	2 oz
canned and drained	225 g	8 oz
Muesli	150 g	5 oz
Noodles - uncooked	75 g	3 oz

Food	Metric	Imperial
Nuts - almonds, whole blanched	150 g	5 oz
- flaked	100 g	4 oz
- ground	90 g	3½ oz
- Brazil, whole shelled	150 g	5 oz
- cashews, whole shelled	150 g	5 oz
- hazelnuts, whole shelled	150 g	5 oz
- peanuts, roasted and salted	150 g	5 oz
- walnuts, halved	100 g	4 oz
Oats - rolled	75 g	3 oz
Olives - green, stuffed	150 g	5 oz
- black	175 g	6 oz
Onions - chopped	150 g	5 oz
Peaches - fresh, sliced	150 g	5 oz
- canned, sliced and drained	225 g	8 oz
Peas - frozen	100 g	4 oz
- split, dried	200 g	7 oz
Peppers - sliced	100 g	4 oz
Potatoes		
- cooked and mashed	225 g	8 oz
Prunes - dried	200 g	7 oz
- cooked and stoned	225 g	8 oz
Raisins - seedless	165 g	5½ oz
Rhubarb - raw sliced	200 g	7 oz
Rice - long grain, uncooked	200 g	7 oz
Rice - short grain, uncooked	215 g	7½ oz
Sago	190 g	6½ oz
Salmon		
- canned, drained and flaked	175 g	6 oz
Semolina	190 g	6½oz

Food	Metric	Imperial
Spaghetti		
- broken, uncooked	100 g	4 oz
Strawberries - fresh whole	150 g	5 oz
Suet - shredded	100 g	4 oz
Sugar - granulated	200 g	7 oz
- caster	200 g	7 oz
- icing	100 g	4 oz
- brown	200 g	7 oz
- demerara	200 g	7 oz
Sultanas	175 g	6 oz
Syrup and treacle	350 g	12 oz
Tapioca	175 g	6 oz
Tomatoes - canned in juice	225 g	8 oz
- fresh, peeled and quartered	150 g	5 oz
Tuna fish		
- canned, drained and flaked	200 g	7 oz

For how to use the following charts see page 56.

CUP AND SPOON REPLACEMENT FOR OUNCES

INGREDIENT	½oz	1 oz	2 oz	3 oz	4 oz	5 oz	6 oz	7 oz	8 oz
Almonds, ground	2T	¼C	½C	¾C	1¼C	1C	1²/₃C	2C	2¼C
silvered	6t	¼C	½C	¾C	1C	1½C	1²/₃C	2C	2¼C
whole	2T	¼C	1/3C	½C	¾C	1C	1¼C	1¹/₃C	1½C
Apples, dried whole	3T	½C	1C	1¹/₃C	2C	2¹/₃C	2¾C	3¹/₃C	3¾C
Apricots, chopped	2T	¼C	½C	¾C	1C	1¼C	1½C	1¾C	2C
whole	2T	3T	½C	²/₃C	1C	1¼C	1¹/₃C	1½C	1¾C
Arrowroot	1T	2T	1/3C	½C	²/₃C	¾C	1C	1¼C	1¹/₃C
Baking Powder	1T	2T	1/3C	½C	²/₃C	¾C	1C	1C	1¼C
Barley	1T	2T	¼C	½C	²/₃C	¾C	1C	1C	1¼C
Bicarbonate of Soda	1T	2T	1/3C	½C	²/₃C	¾C	1C	1C	1¼C
Breadcrumbs, dry	2T	¼C	½C	¾C	1C	1¼C	1½C	1¾C	2C
soft	¼C	½C	1C	1½C	2C	2½C	3C	3²/₃C	4¼C
Biscuit Crumbs	2T	¼C	½C	¾C	1¼C	1¹/₃C	1²/₃C	2C	2¼C
Butter	3t	6t	¼C	1/3C	½C	²/₃C	¾C	1C	1C
Cheese, grated									
lightly packed									
natural cheddar	6t	¼C	½C	¾C	1C	1¼C	1½C	1¾C	2C
Processed cheddar	5t	2T	1/3C	²/₃C	¾C	1C	1¼C	1½C	1²/₃
Parmesan, Romano	6t	¼C	½C	¾C	1C	1¹/₃C	1²/₃C	2C	2¼
Cherries, glace, chopped	1T	2T	1/3C	½C	¾C	1C	1C	1¹/₃C	1½C
whole	1T	2T	1/3C	½C	²/₃C	¾C	1C	1¼C	1¹/₃C
Cocoa	2T	¼C	½C	¾C	1¼C	1¹/₃C	1²/₃	2C	2¼
Coconut, dessicated	2T	1/3C	²/₃C	1C	1¹/₃C	1²/₃C	2C	2¹/₃C	2²/₃C
shredded	1/3C	²/₃C	1¼C	1¾C	2½C	3C	3²/₃C	4¹/₃C	5C
Cornflower	6t	3T	½C	²/₃C	1C	1¼C	1½C	1²/₃C	2C
Coffee, ground	2T	1/3C	²/₃C	1C	1¹/₃C	1²/₃C	2C	2¹/₃C	2²/₃C
instant	3T	½C	1C	1½C	1¾C	2¼C	2²/₃C	3C	3½C
Cornflakes	½C	1C	2C	3C	4¼C	5¼C	6¼C	7½C	8¹/₃C
Cream of Tartar	1T	2T	1/3C	½C	²/₃C	¾C	1C	1C	1¼C

INGREDIENT	½oz	1 oz	2 oz	3 oz	4 oz	5 oz	6 oz	7 oz	8 oz
Currants	1T	2T	$1/3$C	$2/3$C	¾C	1C	1¼C	1½C	1$2/3$C
Custard Powder	6t	3T	½C	$2/3$C	1C	1¼C	1½C	1$2/3$C	2C
Dates, chopped	1T	2T	$1/3$C	$2/3$C	¾C	1C	1¼C	1½C	1$2/3$C
whole pitted	1T	2T	$1/3$C	½C	¾C	1C	1¼C	1½C	1½C
Figs, chopped	1T	2T	$1/3$C	½C	¾C	1C	1C	1$1/3$C	1½C
Flour, plain or self-raising	6t	¼C	½C	¾C	1C	1¼C	1½C	1¾C	2C
wholemeal	6t	3T	½C	$2/3$C	1C	1¼C	1½C	1$2/3$C	1¾C
Fruit, mixed	1T	2T	$1/3$C	½C	¾C	1C	1¼C	1$1/3$C	1½C
Gelatine	5t	2T	$1/3$C	½C	¾C	1C	1C	1¼C	1½C
Ginger, crystallised pieces	1T	2T	$1/3$C	½C	¾C	1C	1¼C	1$1/3$C	1½C
ground	6t	$1/3$C	½C	¾C	1¼C	1½C	1¾C	2C	2¼C
preserved, heavy syrup	1T	2T	$1/3$C	½C	$2/3$C	¾C	1C	1C	1¼C
Glucose, liquid	2t	1T	2T	¼C	$1/3$C	½C	½C	$2/3$C	$2/3$C
Golden Syrup	2t	1T	2T	¼C	$1/3$C	½C	½C	$2/3$C	$2/3$C
Haricot Beans	1T	2T	$1/3$C	½C	$2/3$C	¾C	1C	1C	1¼C
Honey	2t	1T	2T	¼C	$1/3$C	½C	½C	$2/3$C	$2/3$C
Jam	2t	1T	2T	¼C	$1/3$C	½C	½C	$2/3$C	¾C
Lentils	1T	2T	$1/3$C	½C	$2/3$C	¾C	1C	1C	1¼C
Macaroni (see pasta)									
Milk powder, full cream	2T	¼C	½C	¾C	1¼C	1½C	1$2/3$C	2C	2¼C
non fat	2T	$1/3$C	¾C	1¼C	1½C	2C	2$1/3$C	2¾C	3¼C
Nutmeg	6t	3T	½C	$2/3$C	¾C	1C	1¼C	1½C	1$2/3$C
Nuts, chopped	6t	¼C	½C	¾C	1C	1¼C	1½C	1¾C	2C
Oatmeal	1T	2T	½C	$2/3$C	¾C	1C	1¼C	1½C	1$2/3$C
Olives, whole	1T	2T	$1/3$C	$2/3$C	¾C	1C	1¼C	1½C	1$2/3$C
sliced	1T	2T	$1/3$C	$2/3$C	¾C	1C	1¼C	1½C	1$2/3$C
Pasta, short (eg macaroni)	1T	2T	$1/3$C	$2/3$C	¾C	1C	1¼C	1½C	1$2/3$C
Peaches, dried & whole	1T	2T	$1/3$C	$2/3$C	¾C	1C	1¼C	1½C	1$2/3$C
chopped	6t	¼C	½C	¾C	1C	1¼C	1½C	1¾C	2C

INGREDIENT	½oz	1 oz	2 oz	3 oz	4 oz	5 oz	6 oz	7 oz	8 oz
Peanuts, shelled, raw, whole	1T	2T	1/3C	½C	¾C	1C	1¼C	11/3C	1½C
roasted	1T	2T	1/3C	2/3C	¾C	1C	1¼C	1½C	12/3C
Peanut Butter	3t	6t	3T	1/3C	½C	½C	2/3C	¾C	1C
Peas, split	1T	2T	1/3C	½C	2/3C	¾C	1C	1C	1¼C
Peel, mixed	1T	2T	1/3C	½C	¾C	1C	1C	1¼C	1½C
Potato, powder	1T	2T	¼C	1/3C	½C	2/3C	¾C	1C	1¼C
flakes	¼C	½C	1C	11/3C	2C	21/3C	2¾C	31/3C	3¾C
Prunes, chopped	1T	2T	1/3C	½C	2/3C	¾C	1C	1¼C	11/3C
whole pitted	1T	2T	1/3C	½C	2/3C	¾C	1C	1C	1¼C
Raisins	2T	¼C	1/3C	½C	¾C	1C	1C	11/3C	1½C
Rice, short grain raw	1T	2T	¼C	½C	2/3C	¾C	1C	1C	1¼C
long grain raw	1T	2T	1/3C	½C	¾C	1C	1¼C	11/3C	1½C
Rice Bubbles	2/3C	1¼C	2½C	32/3C	5C	6¼C	7½C	8¾C	10C
Rolled Oats	2T	1/3C	2/3C	1C	11/3C	1¾C	2C	2½C	2¾C
Sago	2T	¼C	1/3C	½C	¾C	1C	1C	1¼C	1½C
Salt, common	3t	6t	¼C	1/3C	½C	2/3C	¾C	1C	1C
Semolina	1T	2T	1/3C	½C	¾C	1C	1C	11/3C	1½C
Spices	6t	3T	¼C	1/3C	½C	½C	2/3C	¾C	1C
Sugar crystalline 1A	3t	6t	¼C	1/3C	½C	2/3C	¾C	1C	1C
caster	3t	5t	¼C	1/3C	½C	2/3C	¾C	1C	1¼C
icing	1T	2T	1/3C	½C	¾C	1C	1C	1¼C	1½C
moist brown	1T	2T	1/3C	½C	¾C	1C	1C	11/3C	1½C
Sultanas	1T	2T	1/3C	½C	¾C	1C	1C	1¼C	1½C
Tapioca	1T	2T	1/3C	½C	2/3C	¾C	1C	1¼C	11/3C
Treacle	2t	1T	2T	¼C	1/3C	½C	½C	2/3C	2/3C
Walnuts, chopped	2T	¼C	½C	¾C	1C	1¼C	1½C	1¾C	2C
halved	2T	1/3C	2/3C	1C	1¼C	1½C	1¾C	2¼C	2½C
Yeast, dried	6t	3T	½C	2/3C	1C	1¼C	11/3C	12/3C	1¾C
compressed	3t	6t	3T	1/3C	½C	½C	2/3C	¾C	1C

How to use these charts when converting recipes

't' represents a 5 ml teaspoon
'T' represents a 15 ml tablespoon
'C' represents an American Standard Cup

Find the ingredient you are using in the recipe e.g. caster sugar.

If the American recipe states ½ cup, look along the line until you come to ½ cup and the figure at the top of that column shows that this is the same as 4 oz caster sugar.

Similarly if using currants - 2T is the same as 1 oz currants.

These imperial measures can also be converted to metric measures by referring to the lists on pages 3-4, 57 and 112.

Those who prefer to work in American cups can use the chart the opposite way by finding the Imperial weight the recipe states at the top of the chart and reading the spoon or cup equivalent below.

BRITISH AND AMERICAN VARIATION IN CUPS, SPOONS AND LIQUID MEASURES

British		American
1 teaspoon	equals	1¼ teaspoons
1 tablespoon		1½ tablespoons
¼ pint or 142 ml		$^5/_8$ cup
½ pint or 284 ml		1¼ cups
¾ pint or 426 ml		1$^7/_8$ cups
1 pint or 568 ml		2½ cups

American Measures

1 American cup is equivalent to 8 American fluid ounces
1 American pint equals 16 British fluid ounces
or just over ¾ of a British pint
3 American teaspoons equal 1 American tablespoon
16 American tablespoons equal 1 American cup
2 American tablespoons equal 1 American fluid ounce

Alcoholic Measure

1½ American fluid ounces equals 1 jigger

CHAPTER 5

WEIGHTS AND MEASURES
IN THE AUSTRALIAN KITCHEN

Cookery books and recipes written in magazines for the Australian consumer are now widely available around the world. Australia adopted the metric system of weights and measures many years ago, but their metric measures are different to the metric conversions from Imperial measures in Britain. Instead of adopting 25 grams as equivalent to the Imperial one ounce used in the UK, they use 30 grams as equivalent to one Imperial ounce.

Besides this difference, Australian recipes frequently incorporate cup and spoon measures which are different to American and British cups, so to follow an Australian recipe it is necessary to know what quantity each cup and spoon size represents. The information given here will also enable Australians who have old family recipes written in Imperial measures to 'translate' them into modern Australian measures, so this book will be useful for them as well as British and American consumers being able to enjoy Australian recipes.

DRY MEASURES

(to the nearest 5g)

Ounces		Grams
½	is equivalent to	15
1		30
2		60
3		90
4 (¼ pound)		125
5		155
6		185
7		220

Ounces		Grams
8 oz (½ pound)	is equivalent to	250
9 oz		280
10 oz		315
11 oz		345
12 oz (¾ pound)		375
13 oz		410
14 oz		440
15 oz		470
16 oz (1 pound)		500 (0.5 kg)
24 oz (1½ pounds)		750
32 oz (2 pounds)		1000 (1 kg)
3 pounds		1500 (1.5kg)
4 pounds		2000 (2 kg)

CUP AND SPOON SIZES USED IN AUSTRALIA

CUPS
1 Australian metric cup holds 250 ml
½ Australian metric cup holds 125 ml
$^1/_3$ Australian metric cup holds   83.3 ml
¼ Australian metric cup holds   62.5 ml

SPOONS
1 tablespoon holds 20 ml
1 tablespoon holds 5 ml
½ tablespoon holds 2.5 ml
¼ tablespoon holds 1.25 ml

Note – all cup and spoon measurements are level

AUSTRALIAN LIQUID MEASURES

Fluid Ounce	Millilitres	Cups
1	30	
2	60	
3	100	
4	125	
5 (¼ pint)	150	
6	190	
8	250	1
10 (½ pint)	300	1¼
16	500	2
20 (1 pint)	600	2¹/₈

Because of the difference in measurements, Australian equipment sizes are a bit different too but these sizes can be worked out by using the general conversion figures given in Chapter 9 (page 102).

Oven temperatures are very similar to those in the UK so refer to page 115 for equivalent temperatures for ° F (Fahrenheit), ° C(Centigrade) and Gas Mark.

CHAPTER 6

SHOPPING

OUNCE AND POUND WON'T ALWAYS BE AROUND SO IT IS WISE TO GET KNOWLEDGEABLE WITH METRIC QUANTITIES WHEN SHOPPING

Successful meals start with deciding on a healthy menu, choosing good interesting recipes and incorporating fresh food whenever possible. Any time spent in planning is well worthwhile and even if you can only stop and read a few labels each time you go shopping this is time well spent. It is of course vital if you need to avoid certain foods like nuts, or increase or decrease the intake of a certain food or nutrient to improve your health.

HOW MUCH FOOD SHOULD YOU BUY

The quantity of food bought and served depends on the number being catered for and the occasion. The recommended average quantities of food to serve per portion both for every day meals and entertaining are in Chapter 7.

If you find other information on weights and measures of foods particularly helpful, then jot it down at the back of this book. It is meant to be a working reference book and the more personal notes that are added the more useful it will be. For instance why not make a note of the shopping list for food you used last year at Christmas time. This together with the weight of the chicken or turkey you bought and whether it was too large or small will save a lot of time rethinking all the same things through again.

Everyone wants value for money and so the best and most economical prices need to be worked out. Even if you prefer Imperial pricing, it is wise to get familiar with how to work out the cost of an item in pounds(£) or pence per gram or kilogram. You cannot muddle price per pound with price per kilogram, you must work in one system or the other. The price per ounce or pound or unit is often still shown on a packet or label or shelf, but the print showing the price per gram, kilogram or litre is larger. The maths required to work out the best value of a product is usually much easier to work out in metric. If the food is weighed and displayed that way and the labels show prices per metric weight, a comparison between different products is much easier as you are comparing like with like to get the best value.

There are many legal requirements to which anyone selling anything must conform. These often change but this section gives just a few guidelines to make you aware of how price marking relates to the buying of food using the purchase of fruit and vegetables as examples.

The cost of all food must be indicated prominently either

- near the item itself if it is sold loose e.g. 20p per grapefruit
- on the pack e.g. weight of pack 500 g/price per kg £2.00 – cost of that pack £1.00
- on the edge of the shelf below items sold loose e.g. £2.00 per kilogram

As long as they are clearly displayed, the prices may be listed on a notice very nearby instead of on the product.

To make everything easier for the manufacturer and the consumer, many goods are packaged in multiples of five. For instance a pack of butter which some people may still think of as 8 ounces is now packed in 225 grams. If a mathematical conversion is done, 8 x 28.3495 grams equals 226.796 grams. This figure rounded up comes to 227 grams so the nearest multiple of 5 is 225 grams. In smaller shops or on market stalls, items are rarely pre-packed. All prices displayed should be per kilogram or per 100 gram or per litre or per metre depending on the product. Written alongside may be the cost per pound or per ounce in smaller letters to help those customers who are not familiar with metric weighing and pricing.

However it is far better when deciding what to eat and making a shopping list, to write the amount needed in metric quantities, then neither you or the shop keeper has to convert from one measure to the other and adjust the price accordingly.

A rough guide to how to ask for what you want

If you want a quarter pound (113 g) ask for 100 g which is slightly less.

If you want half a pound (227 g) ask for 225 g which is slightly less.

If you want one pound (454 g) ask for 500 g or half a kilogram which is slightly more.

If you want two pounds (908 g) ask for one kilogram which is slightly more

A GUIDE TO BUYING FRUIT, VEGETABLES AND EGGS

You may prefer to buy fruit and vegetables loose so that you can purchase the amount you desire to suit your needs and check that the items are the correct size and quality you want. For instance you may want to buy four small bananas which are not very ripe.

Loose items such as bananas, apples or a melon should be weighed in metric units in front of each customer and the cost told to you by the cashier at the check-out before you pay. This is called 'countable produce'.

If items such as tomatoes are in a pack of 6 or 8 then the cost per pack can be displayed, not the cost per kg or lb. The number of items in the pack must be clearly visible. However when buying this way you cannot compare prices to find out if the tomatoes in a pack cost more per kilogram than the tomatoes sold 'loose' which have to be priced per kilogram at the check-out.

It is tempting to buy even sized tomatoes in a covered tray as it is a bit quicker if you are in a hurry, but if you can spend a minute or two longer it is easy to choose six tomatoes yourself from the box and usually save some cash.

Pre-packed soft fruits, for example a punnet of strawberries, are also sold by net weight, so the quantity should be made known to the buyer before payment is made.

Some items such as bunches of spring onions, bags of watercress or cloves of garlic do not have to be sold by weight, or have weight markings if pre-packed, provided they are sold by the item.

Buying Potatoes

Pre-packed potatoes must be packed in the following metric prescribed quantities only; 500 g, 1 kg, 1.5 kg, 2 kg, 2.5 kg or a multiple of 2.5 kg up to 15 kg, 20 kg, and 25 kg.

If each potato in a pack weighs over 175g these quantities do not apply. The weight need not be marked provided the number is given and a statement appears stating each potato is over 175 g. This situation could occur when large potatoes for baking are purchased.

A Guide to buying eggs

The use of the correct size egg in a recipe may seem unimportant but in fact it can make quite a difference to the finished result.

Eggs used to be sold in sizes 0 - 7. This has now been changed to the categories shown i.e. small, medium, large and very large. So if you have a recipe with numbers on it instead of sizes, follow this chart.

New Size	Weight	Old Size
Very Large	73g +over	Size 0
		Size 1
Large	63 - 73g	Size 1
		Size 2
		Size 3
Medium	53 - 63g	Size 3
		Size 4
		Size 5
Small	53g + under	Size 5
		Size 6
		Size 7

Each of the categories must fall within 10 grams of the weight band shown above. The Lion Quality Registered Trademark on eggs and egg boxes means that the eggs have been produced to the highest quality standards of food safety. It indicates that they have been produced, held and distributed under best conditions, including animal welfare provisions and environmental policies and their distribution under temperature controlled conditions ensures quality and freshness. All the eggs with this mark are date coded with a 'best before' date. The Lion quality assurance replaces the former Grade quality definitions.

Under European law there are two classes of egg quality: A & B. Grade A eggs are the highest grade. They are naturally clean, fresh eggs, internally perfect with shells intact and the air sac not exceeding 6mm in depth. The yolk must not move away from the centre of the egg on rotation. Grade A eggs are sold as shell eggs. All Class A eggs have to be marked with a code showing the type of farming system, country of origin and production unit.

LABELLING OF FOOD PRODUCTS

This is quite a complex subject and legislation is changing all the time. Just remember that it is important to read labels and the time this takes is well worthwhile. For instance note the *'use by'* and *'best before'* dates especially if you are buying ahead for a self catering holiday or for a special event.

Some foods have a *'Display until'* date which is usually a few days before the *'Use by'* date. Between the *'Display Until'* date and the *'Use By'* date, foods are often reduced in price because after the *'Use By'* date the food has to be removed from sale which means a financial loss to the store. Money can be saved this way by careful shopping.

NUTRITION INFORMATION ON LABELS

In order to be able to choose the most healthy products, or the ones that are most suitable for your nutritional requirements, it is necessary to be able to read the contents label on the packaging. This may be the actual nutrients contained and/or how it has been prepared and cooked, which can alter the nutritional value.

To be able to implement current nutritional advice regarding a healthy diet, the amount of fat, especially saturated fat and sodium (salt) present in the food is important. Other nutrients such as vitamins and minerals may also be stated depending on the food product. How many calories or joules are to be found in one serving of that food may be given, also the number of kilocalories and/or kilojoules present in every 100 g (around 4 oz) of the food are often listed. (See page 129 to convert kilocalories to kilojoules)

VALUE FOR MONEY

Ingredients listed on a label have to be written in descending order, that is the ingredient present in the largest quantity is first on the list of contents. This can give a good idea of the quality of the food. For instance if water is the biggest ingredient, followed by onion and carrot and then meat in a can of stew, the chances are you are not going to get a good amount of meat in each helping.

AVOIDING SOME SUBSTANCES

Many customers require information of what a product does NOT contain. If you have an allergy and are on a diet where you have to avoid for instance gluten, nuts or certain colourings then being able to read the content list on the label is vital. To make this clearer some products are labelled *'free from'* or show a special symbol indicating that it does not contain a certain substance.

'E' NUMBERS AND THEIR MEANING

'E' stands for Europe, and 'E' numbers are a shorthand way of writing down long chemical names of various substances such as additives, colourings, flavourings and preservatives present in the food. By reading the label and noting the number, you can tell just what is present in the food.

All food manufacturers across Europe use the same 'E' number system. So whether you are buying food in Britain, abroad on holiday, or imported, you can buy with confidence. This is especially important for those wishing to avoid a substance. For instance anyone with an allergy to tartrazine colouring (E102) can look at the label to check if that 'E' number is present and avoid that food if it is seen to contain it. It is important to understand that 'E' numbers are not bad substances. Indeed many of them like vitamin C (E300) and vitamin B12 (E101) are natural substances which are found in food. Booklets listing what each E number represents can be bought from bookshops.

STORAGE INFORMATION

This is often shown as a temperature above or below which the food should not be kept if it is to remain good to eat until the *'Use By'* date. Or it may just read *'Keep Refrigerated after opening'* or *'Freeze on day of Purchase'*.

It is important that your refrigerator or freezer is run at the correct temperature to keep all food at its best. (see pages 119 and 125 for refrigerator and freezer information) If the label says *'Suitable for home freezing'* then it is important to freeze it as soon as you get home Wrap and label it suitably with the contents and date. Do not leave it in the kitchen or refrigerator before freezing it and do not re freeze it after defrosting unless it has been cooked first. For instance if some mince is defrosted to make a dish, the cooked dish may then be frozen.

PREPARATION AND COOKING INSTRUCTIONS

Instructions regarding the preparation of the food such as defrosting or the temperature and length of cooking time may also be on a label. These can be vital to enjoy food at its best and safest and should always be followed.

CHAPTER 7

ENTERTAINING

Entertaining to celebrate a particular event ? Don't panic. Whether you are having a small gathering of friends or a large buffet party, your guide to measures and quantities is here.

How many different items should you serve for a buffet and how do you work out how much soup, pâte, canapés, cheese or fruit and so on to allow for each person attending ?

Or perhaps you wish to serve sandwiches. How much butter, spread and filling is required for sandwiches of various kinds for various numbers of people ? How are these sandwiches best wrapped, stored and served.? Will they freeze ?

Perhaps you need to know the size of cake required for a number of people, how large should each of the tiers be for a wedding cake in order for it to be in proportion and what ingredients are needed to make various sizes of fruit cakes. And don't forget the almond paste and icing; quantities for those are given here too.

Having friends around? How many glasses of wine can be poured from one bottle? And finally don't forget the champagne. The number of glasses which can be served from various sized bottles are given.

Knowing the quantities of food required in various situations and how to store them correctly so that you can get ahead with planning and preparation, prevents panic, expensive wastage, or the embarrassment of inadequate supplies.

QUANTITY GUIDE FOR SNACKS OR SMALL PARTY BUFFETS

(all sizes and quantities are approximate)

Bread

1 large sliced loaf (about 2 pound size) provides about 20 slices of bread depending on the thickness they are cut.

Use medium sliced cut for standard sandwiches, thin sliced for rolled sandwiches and thick slices for toast and open sandwiches.

French sticks of standard length can be cut into approximately 20 x 2 cm (1 inch) slices.

Garlic bread

Allow 75 g (3 oz) butter and 1 clove of garlic to each small French loaf and 150 g – 175 g (5 - 6 oz) butter and two small cloves of garlic to each long French loaf.

Butter

100 g (4 oz) creamed butter will butter 20 slices of bread.
225 g (8 oz) creamed butter will butter 24 rolls

Basic Fillings for 12 Rolls or Sandwiches

350 g (12 oz) smoked fish, pâté or meat such as ham or poultry
350 g (12 oz) cream cheese
150 g (6 oz) grated hard cheese
400 g (15 oz) canned tuna fish - drained
150 g (6 oz) pâté de fois gras
10 hard boiled eggs mashed with 50 g (2oz) softened butter
350 g (12 oz) chicken roll or corned beef thinly sliced
250 g (10 oz) salami thinly sliced
225 g (8 oz) cole slaw spread thinly

350 g (12 oz) dressed crab with 150 ml (¼ pint) thick mayonnaise
450 g (1 pound) medium sized tomatoes yield approximately 35 - 40 slices

Allow 2 rounds of sandwiches per head
1-2 savoury pastries per head
2-3 chipolata sausages per head
1-2 small sweet items per head
(see page 76 for freezing sandwiches)

GUIDELINES FOR QUANTITIES TO BUY FOR A LARGE BUFFET

	For 25 people	For 50 people	For 100 people	For 150 people
Bread - sliced	3 loaves	4 loaves	6 loaves	10 loaves
French sticks - long	6	12	24	36
Butter or margarine	900 g	1¾ kg	3¾ kg	5½ kg

(Measures taken to nearest practical quantity)

The amounts listed below are average portion sizes if a variety of food is served. If the choice is limited, for instance the only meat offered is chicken, then the portions should be larger.

SOUP

200ml (⅓ pint) when served as a first course
300ml (½ pint) when served as part of a light lunch with rolls and cheese or similar.

MAIN COURSE - all quantities per person

MEAT   -   100 g (4 oz) when served with a selection of vegetables

      -   175 g – 225 g (6 oz -8 oz) when serving roast meat which needs trimming of fat or chops or joints which includes the weight of the bone

- steaks may be from 100 g to 350 g (4 oz to 12 oz) depending on appetite and the occasion. An average steak will be about 175 g (6 oz)

POULTRY – number of portions served from various kinds and sizes of poultry

Turkey

A 4.5 kg - 6.3 kg (10 - 14 pounds) oven ready turkey will serve 14 people as part of a main meal. It will serve 28 - 30 people if served as cold meat accompanied by other sliced meats and food as in a buffet.

When choosing or ordering a turkey remember that the parts that are discarded during the dressing of the bird to make it ready for the oven can weigh around 1.4 kg - 1.8 kg (3 - 4 pounds). These form part of the total weight and are paid for, even though they are only used for stock. As the turkey carcass is so large it is not profitable to buy a small bird as the amount of meat obtained from it as a percentage of the total cost is very small.

Goose

A 4.5 kg - 5.4 kg (10 - 12 pound) oven ready goose will serve about 8 people.

Duck

A 450 g (1 pound) dressed duck is needed for each portion.
A 1.8 kg - 2.7 kg (4 - 6 pounds) duck as bought will serve 3 - 4 people.
A young duckling weighing 1.6 kg - 1.8 kg (3½ - 4 pounds) will serve two people.

Chicken
Poussins

These are young chicken about 6 - 8 weeks old weighing 450 g – 900 g) (1 - 2 pounds) and one will serve 1 or 2 people

Boilers

These are twelve week old chicken weighing between 1.1 kg - 1.4 kg (2½ - 3 pounds) Each will serve 3 to 4 people.

Large Roasting Chickens

Weighing about 1.8 kg and 2.3 kg (4 - 5 pounds), each bird should serve six or seven people.

Capons

Capons are 10 -12 weeks old and will serve 8 - 10 people. They usually weigh around 2.7 kg - 3.6 kg (6 - 8 pounds)

Guinea Fowl

Guinea fowl are small birds weighing 550 g - 1.7 kg (1¼ - 3¼ pounds) An average sized bird will serve 4 people.

GAME

Grouse

An average sized grouse will serve 1 or 2 portions

Partridge

A young roasted partridge will provide 1 or 2 portions

Quail

One bird per person is served

Pheasant

An average sized pheasant will provide 2 portions, but larger pheasants can be bought to serve 4 people.

FISH

Around 175 g (6 oz) per portion if used in a fish dish. Many fish are sold per item i.e. one trout, one plaice etc so you can choose the size that looks right for your requirements rather than the weight

VEGETABLES AND FRUIT

Per portion   -   225 g (8 oz) of leafy vegetables such as cabbage
                -    100 g (4 oz) root vegetables such as carrots and potatoes
                -    100 g (4 oz) peas, beans, sweetcorn and similar

If a wide selection of vegetables are served then the quantity needed of each will be reduced.

The general rule is that you can eat as much fruits and vegetables as you like and in as large a variety as possible. Five portions a day at least, (not including potatoes) are recommended for good health. Include fresh items whenever possible but some of the '5 a Day' can be dried fruit, or dried peas, beans or lentils. (See page 99-100 for cooking pulses)

In weight this means around 400 grams - 450 grams (about 1 pound) of fruit or vegetables a day, each of the five portions weighing about 80 grams (3 - 3½ ounces). There is no need to actually weigh each piece. One portion is about one apple, one banana, one orange or a similar item of fruit, or an average helping of pure orange juice, carrots, beans, green vegetables or similar.

Local produce eaten soon after it is picked or dug up cannot be beaten for goodness and flavour.

RICE AND PASTA - allow an average of 50 g (2 oz) dry weight per portion. 275 g (10 oz) uncooked weight will serve 6 people. 550 g (1¼ pounds) serves 10 people

QUICHE - one 20 cm (8 inch) diameter will serve 6 portions. Two this size will serve 10 portions

PÂTE - allow 50 g (2oz) per person

CHEESE BOARD - allow 25 g/ 50 g (1- 2 oz) per person

SAVOURY SAUCES served separately in a sauce boat - 50 ml (2 fl oz) per portion

SWEET SAUCES LIKE CUSTARD - 75 ml (3 fl oz) per person. 450 ml (1 pint) will serve 8-10 portions

FRUIT SALAD - home made is best, using at least 5 varieties of fruit - whatever is in season. If canned is used, then an 820 g (1¾ pound) tin will serve about 20 people.

STEWED FRUIT - 500 g (1 pound) for every 4 portions

CAKES
Sponge Cake - 1 x 18 cm (7 inch) diameter sponge cuts into 6-8 portions
Round Cake - 1 x 22 cm (9 inch) diameter round cake cuts into 20 slices
Square Cake - 1 x 22 cm (9 inch) square cake cuts into 54 smallish slices

WEDDING CAKES
450 g (1 pound) cooked mixture provides 8 - 10 portions as each portion is small and not as large as a normal portion of cake. (See page 88-91 for cake sizes and mixtures for cakes, almond paste and icing)

AMOUNTS TO SERVE PER GUEST
As an average guide, serve 6 - 8 savoury items and 2 sweet items per guest if the gathering such as a wedding reception is in the afternoon.

If the reception is at lunch time more substantial fare such as a meal will be needed. For an evening party serve more buffet items.

STORAGE, FREEZING AND THAWING TIMES FOR SANDWICHES

Whether for packed lunches, a small gathering or a large party, planning ahead can save a lot of time and bother, for instance having sandwiches ready prepared in the freezer.

All varieties of bread can be frozen but crisp/crusty breads such as French sticks are liable to lose their crispness when thawed.

Fillings which are not suitable for freezing are hard boiled eggs - they become rubbery, also foods with a high water content such as mayonnaise, and salad items like lettuce and cucumber. Add these at the last moment after the sandwich has been defrosted.

If you prefer, fillings can be prepared and frozen separately from the bread, and the sandwiches made up near to the time of eating. Pack the spreads into sealed polythene containers, label carefully and keep for 1-2 months depending on the filling. Leave frozen fillings to defrost at room temperature for 2-3 hours or overnight in a refrigerator before using.

To Freeze Sandwiches

They may be made and finished ready to serve but it is often better to freeze them in large squares or rolls and cut them up after defrosting. Leave the crusts on and then as the sandwiches defrost, just before serving them, cut them into the shapes desired, remove crusts if wished and garnish appropriately.

Wrapping and packing

Wrap in foil or cling film.

Label with the type of filling or spread, the quantity and the date.

Items such as asparagus rolls are best packed closely and frozen together on a tray to prevent them unrolling. Seal with foil.

Freeze pinwheels, club and ribbon sandwiches uncut, wrap tightly in foil and cut just before serving.

Sandwiches may be packed individually if they are likely to be used for a lunch box. Stacks of sandwiches with the same filling may be packed together with cling film between them. Each sandwich can then be unwrapped and defrosted separately as required.

To prevent items breaking in the freezer it is wise to pack them into an icecream container or similar plastic box and wedge them in to keep their shape.

Storage Time

All sandwiches should freeze well for about 2 months depending on the filling.

To Thaw Sandwiches

Thaw them still in their packaging. They are best thawed slowly at room temperature or overnight in a refrigerator. Individual sandwiches will thaw quicker than a large packet.

Approximate thawing times are -

2 hours for individually wrapped sandwiches
6 - 7 hours for stacks of 4 - 6 sandwiches
4 - 5 hours for rolled sandwiches
3 - 4 hours for pinwheels, club and ribbon sandwiches which cut more easily when partially thawed

Toasted Sandwiches

Place frozen, unwrapped sandwiches under a hot grill and they thaw whilst toasting.

BEVERAGES
Non-alcoholic beverages

Tea	40 g (1½ oz) loose tea per gallon of water, depending on the variety of tea and the strength of brew required.
Milk	1.1 litre (2 pints) per 4.5 litres (1 gallon) of tea approximately 28 ml (1 fl.oz) of milk is required per cup

Ground Coffee	225 g - 275 g (8-10 oz) per 4.5 litres (1 gallon) of water
Instant Coffee	50 g - 75 g (2 - 2½ oz) per 4.5 litres (1 gallon) of water
Milk/cream	25 ml (1fl oz) per cup although many guests will probably prefer it black

Wine, spirits and soft drink guide
Servings per bottle

Note - the number of servings obtained from a bottle depends a great deal on the size of the glasses and the generosity of the pourer. Therefore the quantities below can only be an average guide.

Sherry	12 - 15 per 70cl bottle
Spirits	24 - 32 per 70cl bottle
Port	12 - 15 per 75cl bottle
Vermouth	12 - 16 per 75cl bottle
Liquors	32 per bottle
Wine	6 per 75cl bottle
Champagne	6 per bottle
Sparkling Wine	6 per 75cl bottle
Cokes	1 can per person

1 pint (568 ml) fruit juice serves 4 - 6 glasses
1 bottle fruit squash when diluted serves between 20 - 26 glasses

Champagne

Champagne is in a class of its own and the bottle capacities have special names

		litre capacity
1 bottle		0.75
1 Magnum equivalent to	2 bottles	1.5
1 Jeroboam	4 bottles	3.0
1 Rohoboam	6 bottles	4.5
1 Mathusalem	8 bottles	6.0
1 Salmanazar	12 bottles	9.0
1 Balthazar	16 bottles	12.0
1 Nebuchadnezzar	20 bottles	15.0

CHAPTER 8

COOKING

This book is not a cookery book, but in this chapter you will find *basic* information on weights, measurements, temperatures and cooking times which are the practical help you need when preparing certain foods. It forms an easy quick reference to various basic cooking procedures so you get good results and avoid waste.

For instance; you want to make a fruit pie for six people. What size pie dish is appropriate and how much pastry will be required to cover it?

Fancy some eclairs. How much flour should you start with to make ten eclairs and how much cream will be needed to fill them ? And what about mince pies, the quantities of pastry needed and amount of mincemeat required to fill them. Similar guidance will be found here for other dishes incorporating pastry also rich fruit cake and sauces.

It is important that meat and poultry should be cooked at the correct temperature, and pulses need special attention to ensure they are cooked through as they can be dangerous to eat. These are expained on page 99.

PASTRY

Nothing can beat homemade pastry, but working out which type to make and how much to make in various situations can be confusing. Making the wrong quantity can lead to the pastry being insufficient to cover a pie dish adequately or having so much pastry over that you make a batch of jam tarts you don't really want.

To calculate the amount of pastry needed

Home made

If a recipe requires a stated amount of pastry this refers to the quantity of flour used to make the pastry e.g. if you need 225 g (8 oz) shortcrust pastry then you need to start with 225 g (8 oz) flour.

Bought pastry

To calculate the amount of pre-prepared bought pastry needed for the same results, add together the weights of flour, fat and water used to make the pastry from a basic recipe e.g.

Bought Shortcrust pastry

225 g (8 oz) flour + 100 g (4 oz) fat + water = approximately 350 g (14 oz) prepared pastry.

Bought puff pastry - To make the same item from pre-prepared puff pastry you will need to buy -

225 g (8 oz) flour + 225 g (8 oz) fat + water = approximately 500 g (1¼ lb) prepared puff pastry.

As a general rule you need just over half as much again in weight if bought pastry is used.

QUANTITY OF PASTRY REQUIRED TO COVER AND/OR LINE VARIOUS SIZE DISHES

All measures and yields are approximate

SHORTCRUST PASTRY

Dish	Size	Pastry quantity
Oval pie dish	½ litre (1 pint) dish	125 g (5 oz) covers
	750 ml (1½ pint) dish	150 g (6 oz) covers
	1 litre (2 pint) dish	225 g (8 oz) covers
	1½ litre (3 pint) dish	250 g (10 oz) covers

Dish	Size		Pastry quantity
Pie plate	18 cm	(7 inch) plate	125 g (5 oz) lines OR covers
	22 cm	(9 inch) plate	150 g (6 oz) lines OR covers
	18 cm	(7 inch) plate	225 g (8 oz) lines AND covers
	22 cm	(9 in) plate	250 g (10 oz) lines AND covers
Tarts	225 g	(8oz) pastry	makes 18 x 6 cm (2½ in) tarts OR 12 x 8 cm (3 in) tarts

FLAN PASTRY

100 g	(4 oz)	flan	pastry lines a	15 cm	(6 inch)	flan ring
125 g	(5 oz)		lines an	18 cm	(7 inch)	flan ring
150 g	(6 oz)		lines a	20 cm	(8 inch)	flan ring OR
			lines a	15 cm	(6 inch)	flan ring AND makes 6 x 6 cm (2½ inch) tartlet cases
200 g	(7 oz)		lines a	20.5 cm	(8 inch)	flan ring
250 g	(9 oz)		lines a	23 cm	(9 inch)	flan ring

The above amounts also apply if shortcrust pastry is used.

PUFF PASTRY

Item	Pastry	Yield
Oval pie dish	100 g (4 oz)	covers one x 1 litre (2 pint) dish
Sausage rolls	225 g (8 oz)	makes twelve x 8 cm (3 inch) rolls

Sausage rolls made from the above quantity require 225 g (8 oz) of sausage meat for filling.

Item	Pastry	Yield
Vol au vents	225 g (8 oz)	makes twelve x 8 cm (3 inch) (round or oval) OR ten x 9 cm (3½ inch)
	500 g (1 lb)	makes thirty x 8 cm (3 inch) OR twenty x 9 cm (3½ inch)
Bouchées	225 g (8 oz)	makes thirty x 5 cm (2 inch) (round shaped)
	500 g (1 lb)	makes sixty x 5 cm (2 inch)
Cream horns	225 g (8 oz)	makes about 10 if the pastry is rolled out to a 25 cm x 45 cm (10 in x 18 in) oblong and rolled ¼ cm or (1/8 inch) thick

When using bought puff pastry, roll it out a bit thinner than you would home made pastry; about 0.2 cm - 0.4 cm (1/16 - 1/8 inches) as it rises very well and you don't want it too thick.

Mince pies each about 6.5 cm (2½ inches) diameter made from 350 g (12 oz) shortcrust or flaky pastry need 350 g - 450 g (about ¾ - 1 pound) mincemeat for filling.

SUET PASTRY

Item	Pastry	Yield
Dumplings	225 g (8 oz)	makes 16 medium dumplings
Suet pudding	225 g (8 oz)	lines and covers a 750 ml (1½ pint) pudding basin
	300 g (12 oz)	lines and covers a 1.4 litre (2½ pint) pudding basin
Roly-poly pudding	225 g (8 oz)	makes 1 x 30.5 cm (12 inch) roll from pastry rolled out to a 25 cm x 30 cm (10 inch x 12 inch) rectangle

CHOUX PASTRY

Item	Pastry	Yield
Eclairs	65 g (2½ oz) flour	makes 10 eclairs each 10 cm (4 in) long OR 25 eclairs each 4 cm (1½ in) long
Choux Buns	65 g (2½ oz) flour	makes 10 buns each 5 cm (2 in) diameter
Profiteroles	65 g (2½ oz) flour	makes 20 each 3 cm (1¼ in) diameter

Each of the above recipes for eclairs, choux buns and profiteroles require 142 ml (¼ pint) (5 fl oz) of double cream, whipped with 4 tbs (60 ml) single cream or top of the milk for the filling.

MINCE PIES OR OTHER FILLED TARTS

Guide for quantities of shortcrust pastry and mincemeat required to make batches of mince pies.

Number of pies each 6 cm (2½ ins) diameter	Weight of pastry required		Mincemeat required
	Homemade pastry	Prepared pastry	
10	225 g (8 oz)	400 g (14 oz)	225 g (8 oz)
20	400 g (1 lb)	700 g (1½ lb)	450 g (1 lb)
50	1 kg (2 lb)	1.5 kg (3½ lb)	1 kg (2¼ lb)

BASIC CAKE MIXES

There are hundreds of cake recipes to be found in hundreds of recipe books and magazines. Two recipes are given here because they are good examples of how basic quantities and measures can be adapted. It can be seen that whichever method of measurement is used and whether 100g OR 115g is suggested as equivalent to 4 ounces, the important thing is that the *proportions* of flour, sugar and fat are the same. This matters in baking more than the actual quantity of ingredient used. In contrast, if you are making a casserole the actual amounts do not matter. The ingredients listed are really just a guide, you can add more carrot if wished and omit celery if you haven't any and so on.

Cakes vary a great deal, but a good recipe gives the exact size of tin required and the oven temperature in degrees Celsius. (For comparative temperatures of ovens see page 115, and for tin sizes see pages 105-108)

VICTORIA SANDWICH

This sponge cake can be enjoyed on its own or used as a base for several cakes and puddings such as a trifle.

The standard basic recipe is —

100g (4oz) sugar
100g (4oz) margarine
2 eggs
100g (4oz) flour

This mixture will fill two 18 cm (7 inch) sandwich tins, or two 15 cm (6 inch) cake tins for deeper cakes, or put all the mixture in one tin 20 cm (8 inch) for one much deeper cake.

This amount of mixture can also be cooked satisfactorily in a Swiss roll tin or will make about 14 small cakes cooked in patty cases.

For a bigger sponge use —

175 g (6 oz) sugar
175 g (6 oz) margarine

3 eggs
175 g (6 oz) flour

This mixture will fit into two 20 cm (8 inch) sandwich tins or one 20 cm (8 inch) cake tin.

Simple steps to follow –
Prepare the cake tin as given in the recipe.

Cream the fat and sugar until pale and fluffy.

Add the egg a little at a time, beating well after each addition.

Fold in half the flour with a metal spoon, then fold in the remainder.

Place half the mixture in each tin.

Bake both cakes on the same shelf of the oven.

Bake at 190°C (375°F) (gas mark 5) for about 20 minutes, or until they are risen, firm to touch and are shrinking away from the sides of the tins. A sharp knife inserted into the centre of the sponge should come out clean.

Cool on a wire rack before sandwiching them together with jam or cream or use them in a dessert such as a trifle.

RICH FRUIT CAKE
Fruit cakes can be required in all shapes and sizes from small birthday cakes to large wedding cakes. The chart on page 88 gives the quantities of ingredients required the cooling time and portions served, from all sizes of this basic recipe whatever the chosen size or shape..

Whatever the chosen recipe these are the simple steps to follow.

Sift the flour and spices together.

In a separate bowl, cream together the fat and sugar till light and fluffy

Beat in the eggs one at a time with a little of the flour to prevent the mixture curdling.

Fold in the remaining flour, the fruit and lemon rind.

Turn the mixture into the prepared tin, smooth the surface and then make a slight hollow in the centre top.

Cook at 140° C (275° F) (gas mark 1) for the time shown on the chart.

About twenty minutes before the end of the cooking time, test to see how the cake is doing, just in case your oven is a bit hotter than it should be and the cake is cooking quicker than expected. The cake is done when a fine bladed knife inserted into the centre of the cake comes out clean. Allow the cake to cool thoroughly in the tin before turning it out onto a wire cooling rack. Make sure it is really cold before wrapping and storing it.

WEDDING CAKES

A rich, dark, fruit cake is traditional for a wedding cake but a lighter fruit cake, a sponge cake or chocolate cake is perfectly acceptable if preferred. Consider carefully how the cake is to be presented. If you wish to have the cake in tiers with pillars between each tier then make sure that the cake is not so soft that the pillars sink into the cake below as it is 'built up'. This can easily happen if a chocolate cake is chosen. If choosing a tiered cake it is also important that the size of each tier is correct, so that when assembled, the whole cake is in proportion and doesn't look top heavy.

Three tier cake

The most favoured sizes for a three tier cake are -
30.5 cm (12 inches) for the bottom tier
23 cm (9 inches) for the middle tier and
15 cm (6 inches) for the top tier.

Ingredients for a Fruit Cake per Size of Tin

Round tin	15 cm	18 cm	20 cm	23 cm	25 cm	28 cm	30 cm	
Square tin	12.5 cm	15 cm	18 cm	20 cm	23 cm	25 cm	28 cm	30 cm
*glacé cherries	65 g	75 g	100 g	150 g	200 g	250 g	350 g	375 g
plain flour	175 g	200 g	250 g	300 g	450 g	600 g	725 g	825 g
currants	150 g	175 g	225 g	275 g	400 g	525 g	675 g	750 g
sultanas	200 g	250 g	350 g	425 g	600 g	800 g	1 kg	1.1 kg
raisins	75 g	75 g	100 g	150 g	200 g	275 g	350 g	400 g
*mixed peel	50 g	50 g	50 g	75 g	100 g	150 g	175 g	200 g
*chopped nuts	25 g	25 g	50 g	75 g	75 g	100 g	175 g	175 g
butter	150 g	175 g	225 g	275 g	400 g	525 g	675 g	750.g
caster sugar	150 g	175 g	225 g	275 g	400 g	525 g	675 g	750 g
eggs	150 g	175 g	225 g	275 g	400 g	525 g	675 g	750 g

Round tin	6 in	7 in	8 in	9 in	10 in	11 in	12 in	
Square tin	5 in	6 in	7 in	8 in	9 in	10 in	11 in	12 in
*glacé cherries	2½ oz	3 oz	4 oz	5 oz	7 oz	9 oz	12 oz	13 oz
plain flour	6 oz	7 oz	9 oz	11 oz	1lb	1 lb 5 oz	1 lb 10 oz	1 lb 13 oz
currants	5 oz	6 oz	8 oz	10 oz	14 oz	1 lb 3 oz	1½ lb	1 lb 11 oz
sultanas	7½ oz	9 oz	12 oz	15 oz	1 lb 5 oz	1 lb 12 oz	2 lb 4 oz	2½ lb
raisins	2½ oz	3 oz	4 oz	5 oz	7 oz	10 oz	12 oz	14 oz
*mixed peel	2 oz	2 oz	2 oz	3 oz	4 oz	5 oz	6 oz	7 oz
*chopped nuts	1 oz	1 oz	2 oz	3 oz	3 oz	4 oz	6 oz	6 oz
butter	5 oz	6 oz	8 oz	10 oz	14 oz	1 lb 3 oz	1½ lb	1 lb 11 oz
caster sugar	5 oz	6 oz	8 oz	10 oz	14 oz	1 lb 3 oz	1½ lb	1 lb 11 oz
eggs	5 oz	6 oz	8 oz	10 oz	14 oz	1 lb 3 oz	1½ lb	1 lb 11 oz

Cooking time (hrs)	3¾	3¾	4	4½	4½	5	5	5
No of slices	25	35	45	60	80	100	120	140

* Optional: If one of these ingredients is not used, the weight can be made up by increasing any of he other fruits.

Two tier cake

A two tier cake can be -
30.5 cm (12 inches) for the bottom tier
20.5 cm (8 inches) for the top tier

OR

25.5 cm (10 inches) for the bottom tier
15 cm (6 inches) for the top tier

In order not to look too heavy the depth of the cakes must also be in proportion, with the bottom tier deeper than the middle and top tiers.

Depths of cakes

The bottom tier should be a minimum 7.5 cm (3 inches) deep.
Cakes which are 18 cm - 23 cm (7 inches - 9 inches) in diameter should be 6.5 cm (2½ inches) deep.

Cakes which are 15 cm (6 inches) diameter should be 5 cm (2 inches) deep.

Each cake should be placed on a board *at least* 2.5 cm (1 inch) *larger* than the bottom tier of the cake. An even larger board will allow for extra icing decoration or flowers to be placed around the base of the cake.

Portions of cake

From each 450 g (1 pound) of cooked mixture you can cut 8 -10 portions of cake. A traditional recipe is very rich and it is not usual to serve large slices at a wedding as you would if you were having friends to tea.

To Cut the Cake

Whether round or square -
Cut the cake in half
Cut this large wedge into thick slices about 5 cm (2 inches) wide.
Cut each of these slices into 1 cm (½ inch) slices

Almond Paste

Home-made almond paste or marzipan tastes especially good.

To make approximately 450 g (1 pound) almond paste the following ingredients are required -

450 g (1 pound) ground almonds
225 g (8 oz) icing sugar
225 g (8 oz) caster sugar
2 large eggs
½ teaspoon vanilla or almond essence
½ teaspoon lemon juice - sufficient to make a stiff dough consistency.
Halve or double these ingredients as necessary for the cake you are covering. (see chart on page 91)

Royal Icing

Royal icing is traditional for any good cake especially a wedding cake.

To make 900 g (2 lb) of Royal icing the following ingredients are required -

900 g (2 lb) icing sugar
4 egg whites
1 tablespoon glycerine (optional)

Halve or double these ingredients as required for the size cake you are decorating.

The glycerine gives the icing a smoother texture and makes it easier to cut without cracking. Extra quantities of icing will be required for the decoration. The amount depends on how elaborate the decoration is, whether a lot of extra icing decoration is placed around the base and the number of icing sugar flowers, trellis, shells etc desired. Use the following guides to make enough almond paste and icing to cover all over each cake with one layer. Halve or double as required. (See chart on page 91)

Size of cake		Amount of almond paste needed	Amount of Royal icing needed
15 cm	(6 in) round	450 g (1 pound)	450 g (1 pound)
15 cm	(6in) square		
18 cm	(7in) round	550 g (1¼ pound)	700 g (1½ pound)
18 cm	(6in) square		
20.5 cm	(8 in) round	675 g (1½ pound)	700 g (1½ pound)
20.5 cm	(7 in) square		
23 cm	(9in) round	800 g (1¾ pound)	900 g (2 pound)
23 cm	(8in) square		
25.5 cm	(10in) round	900 g (2 pound)	1 kg (2¼ pound)
25.5 cm	(9 in) square		
28. cm	(11in) round	1 kg (2¼ pound)	1.1 kg (2½ pound)
28. cm	(10in) square		
30.5 cm	(12in) round	1.1 kg (2½ pound)	1.4 kg (3 pound)
30.5 cm	(11in) square	1.4 kg (3 pound)	1.6 kg (3½ pound)

CHEESECAKE BASES

To make a biscuit base allow 175 g (6 oz) crushed biscuits and 75 g (3 oz) butter or margarine mixed well together to line the base of a 20 cm (8 inch) flan ring or cake tin.

YORKSHIRE PUDDING

Make a batter using -
300 ml (½ pint) milk
100 g (4 oz) flour
1 egg

This will make 6 individual Yorkshire puddings or 12 if they are cooked in small patty tins. These quantities will also make 6 average sized pancakes

BASIC WHITE SAUCE (BECHAMEL SAUCE)

For a **pouring sauce** use –
15 g (½ oz) flour
15 g (½ oz) fat
300 ml (½ pint) liquid, usually all milk

For a **coating sauce** use -
25 g (1oz) flour
25 g (1oz) fat
300 ml (½ pint) liquid

For a **thick sauce** to bind foods use -
50 g (2oz) flour
50 g (2oz) fat
300 ml (½ pint) liquid

Melt the fat, stir in the flour until it thickens to form what is called a roux, then gradually stir in the liquid while over the heat and beat till smooth.

SUGAR AND SWEETS

Sweets are made from a sugar mixture which has been boiled to a high temperature. The temperature required during preparation depends on the type of finished sweet desired.

Making sugar products, sweets and caramel

The basic process is to dissolve sugar in water in a pan and then slowly bring the mixture to the desired temperature according to the recipe for the finished product one is making. As the temperature rises so the liquid evaporates off from the pan, causing a syrup to form and thicken. This becomes darker as the temperature rises. It is very dark brown caramel when it reaches 175°C (350°F)

Thermometers

It is advisable to use a special sugar thermometer to ensure success. It should be graduated from 16°C (60°F) to 182°C (360°F). They are usually made in brass and have a hook at the top from which the thermometer can be suspended into the sugar mixture. Homely tests can be used if you do not have a thermometer.

The Cold Water Test

Care must be taken not to burn your fingers when using homely tests. Drop a teaspoon of toffee into a saucer of cold water and if it immediately sets into a soft pliable ball the toffee is ready.

Check results on the chart below.

Sugar Temperature Chart

Stage	Temperature	Sweet	Cold Water Test
soft ball	115 – 120°C (235°F – 245°F)	fudge and fondants	Firm enough to form into a pliable ball and flatten when pressed between thumb and forefinger
firm ball	120°C – 130°C (245°F – 265°F)	caramel marshmallows soft nougat	Firm pliable and sticky when pressed

Stage	Temperature	Sweet	Cold Water Test
soft crack	135°C – 140°C (280°F – 290°F)	chewy toffee	Holds its shape but is still pliable, not brittle when a little is dropped into iced water
very brittle hardcrack	150°C – 154°C (300°F – 310°F)	hard toffee rock	When a drop of syrup is put into cold water it separates into threads which are hard and brittle
caramel	165°C (335°F)	spun sugar	The threads falling from the spoon will snap. Should be a light brown colour

Different kinds of sugar are used for different sweets, fondants and fudges, and individual recipes should be followed for these.

To make a standard syrup

Place 450 g (1 pound) granulated sugar in a saucepan and add 300 ml (½ pint) water. Bring to the boil and boil steadily until it reaches 105°C (220° F). At this stage when a little of the *cooled* syrup is rubbed between the thumb and forefinger it should feel smooth. Leave the syrup to cool thoroughly and then store it in a clean, dry, screw topped jar.

Caramel

To make basic caramel for a pudding such as a Caramel Custard, dissolve 100 g (4 oz) sugar in 150 ml (¼ pint) water over a low heat. Bring to the boil without stirring until it gradually turns a rich golden brown colour. Transfer carefully to the required tin or use to coat the surface of a dessert.

OVEN TEMPERATURES AND COOKING TIMES FOR ROASTING MEAT AND POULTRY

For good health as well as good texture and flavour it is important that food is cooked at the correct temperature. This applies especially to meat.

Oven temperatures are usually no longer given in Fahrenheit in Britain but they have been included here with the Centigrade and Gas Mark conversion figures, as old recipes and recipes from abroad often still give degrees Fahrenheit in the instructions. This will enable any recipe to be cooked satisfactorily.

Beef - rare	200°C (400° F) gas mark 6	20 minutes per 0.5 kg plus 20 minutes extra
- medium	200° C (400° F) gas mark 6	25 minutes per 0.5 kg plus 25 minutes extra
- well done	200° C (400° F) gas mark 6	30 minutes per 0.5 kg plus 30 minutes extra
Pork	190° C (375° F) gas mark 5	35 minutes per 0.5 kg plus 35 minutes extra
Lamb	190°C (375° F) gas mark 5	25 minutes per 0.5 kg plus 25 minutes extra
Poultry	190° C (375° F) gas mark 5	20 minutes per 0.5 kg plus 20 minutes extra

Note 0.5 kg is equivalent to just over one pound

The temperatures and timings listed above are only guidelines as the tenderness of the meat and the preference for the degree to which it is rare varies. Food and cookers vary also, so to test the food to see if it is cooked through before serving, pierce the thickest part of the meat with a thin bladed knife. Any juices running out of it should be clear and not pink.

It is important that turkeys are thoroughly thawed before being cooked. (For thawing times for turkeys see page 127)

ROASTING TIMES FOR TURKEY

Weight		Cooking Times in Hours	
		160°C (325° F) Gas mark 3 (slow method)	230°C (450°F) Gas mark 8 (quick method)
kg	lbs	hours	hours
2.7 - 3.6	6 - 8	1½ - 3	2¼ - 2½
3.6 - 4.5	8 - 10	3½ - 3¾	2½ - 2¾
4.5 - 5.4	10 - 12	3¾ - 4¼	2¾ - 3
5.4 - 6.3	12 - 14	4 - 4¼	3 - 3¼
6.3 - 7.3	14 - 16	4¼ - 4½	3¼ - 3½
7.3 - 8.2	16 - 18	4½ - 4¾	3½ - 3¾
8.2 - 9.0	18 - 20	4¾ - 5½	3¾ - 4
9.0 - 10.8	20 - 24	4¼ - 5½	4 - 4¼

RECOMMENDED TEMPERATURES OF FAT FOR DEEP FRYING VARIOUS FOODS

Importance of correct fat temperature

The temperature of the fat is important. If it is too hot then the outside of the food will brown and cook on the outside but the inside will be uncooked. If the fat is not hot enough then the food will become soggy as it will absorb the fat, will take a long time to cook and the outside will not turn crispy and brown.

Healthy Frying

For good health, use oil for frying rather than hard fat such as lard or dripping. There are many varieties of oil which can add extra flavour to the food.

Chips

Chips are best blanched first at a lower temperature to cook them. Drain the oil from them, then just before serving immerse them in fat at a high temperature to brown them quickly and give them a crispy texture.

Large, plain cut chips are more healthy than small, thin chips as there is less surface area in contact with the fat during cooking, therefore reducing the amount of fat absorbed and eaten.

The bread test is a simple way of finding out whether the fat is hot enough when you don't have a proper fat thermometer.

If a 2.5 cm (1 inch) cube of bread turns brown when left in the fat for 45 seconds then the fat will be at a temperature of around 190°C (375 °F). It is advisable to use this test to ensure a good result for any of the dishes described below.

Food	Oil Temperature	Bread Test 2.5 cm(1 inch) cube
Uncooked mixtures (doughnuts, fritters etc)	180° C (360°F)	1 minute
Egg and crumbed fish cakes, croquettes and whitebait	190° C (375°F)	45 seconds
Fish fillets and fish in batter	185° C (370°F)	40 seconds
Potatoes/chips blanching until soft	180° C (350° F)	1 minute
frying until crisp and brown	200° C (390°F)	30 seconds
Scotch Eggs	180° C (360°F)	1 minute

Cook the food so it is crispy and not soft from absorbed fat. Allow the food to drain well on kitchen paper to remove as much fat as possible and allow it to crisp up before being served.

PULSES

There are many varieties of peas and beans and although there are many similarities, many require different soaking and cooking times. Most, if not all, pulses can be bought ready cooked in cans. These should be rinsed under cold water before being used in salads or incorporated into recipes. Canned varieties are very convenient but are a more expensive way of eating pulses especially if they are eaten frequently.

MEASURES OF DRIED PULSES

Dried Weight per Portion

Dried beans such as butter beans, haricot beans and kidney beans, also peas, lentils and split peas - allow 25 g – 50 g (1 - 2 ounces) dry weight per person depending on size of appetite and what else is being served.

If dried beans are being served as a vegetable accompaniment to a meat dish, then 25 g (1oz) dry weight per portion is sufficient.

A vegetarian using beans as a main dish should use 50g/75g (2 - 3 oz) dry weight per portion.

Soaking Preparation

Dried pulses, except lentils and split peas, need to be soaked for varying lengths of time.

Overnight

They can be soaked overnight if you have planned your meals far enough ahead.

Cold water soak

Place the pulses in a large pan with a lot of water, and leave to soak for 6 - 8 hours.

Hot water soak

Place pulses in a large pan with a lot of water, bring to the boil, boil for 2 minutes, remove from the heat and leave to soak in the same water for 45 - 60 minutes until cold. Then they can be drained and cooked (see cooking chart on page 100).

Soaking Pulses in the Microwave

To each 100 g (4oz) beans or peas in the bowl add 425 ml (¾ pint) hot water. Cover and heat on full power for about 4 minutes until boiling. Cook for a further 3 minutes on high power then leave to soak for at least an hour. After this time rinse the beans very well again in several changes of cold water. They are now ready to cook.

Cooking

Place the prepared pulses in a large saucepan with lots of cold fresh water. The addition of 30 ml (2 tbs) oil to the water will prevent the beans from foaming and will give them a glossy appearance. Bring the water to the boil and boil rapidly for 10 minutes which will destroy any toxins which may be present in some beans especially red kidney beans.

NOTE - IT IS ESSENTIAL THAT BEANS FROM THE KIDNEY BEAN FAMILY ARE FAST BOILED FIRST FOR AT LEAST 10 MINUTES TO REMOVE TOXINS. AFTER THIS TIME THEY CAN BE COOKED FOR THE REMAINING TIME AS GIVEN.

After the ten minute boiling time if this is required, or after soaking and rinsing, place the peas or beans into a large saucepan with lots of cold fresh water. Bring the water to the boil and boil rapidly for at least 2 minutes.

Then lower the heat and follow the chart overleaf for cooking times. These can vary a bit according to the freshness of the beans.

Cooking times

Aduki beans	1	-	1½ hours
Black beans	1	-	1½ hours
Black eyed peas	25	-	30 minutes
Butter beans	45	-	60 minutes
Cannellini beans	1	-	1½ hours
Chick peas	1	-	2 hours
Flageolet beans	30	-	60 minutes
Haricot beans	1	-	1½ hours
Lentils - brown	25	-	30 minutes
- split red	20	-	30 minutes
Mung beans	25	-	30 minutes
whole peas	45	-	60 minutes
Red kidney beans	1	-	1¼ hours
Soya beans	1	-	3 hours
Split peas	25	-	30 minutes

Cooking in a Microwave

Cover the bowl with film or a loose fitting lid and cook on High (Full Power) for 30 minutes. Leave to stand for 10 minutes, remove lid, drain, rinse and drain again before serving.

Cooking beans in a Pressure Cooker

A pressure cooker is excellent for cooking pulses since it saves a lot of time.

Allow 1.1 litres (2 pints) fresh cold water to every 450 g (1 lb) beans. Bring the water to boiling point and add the beans. Bring to the boil again, uncovered, and remove any scum from the top. Put on the lid and cook for the required time.

Type of Bean	Cooking time at High - 15 lb pressure
Aduki beans	10 minutes
Black eyed peas	20 minutes
Butter beans	25 minutes
Cannellini beans	15 minutes
Chick peas	20 minutes
Flageolet beans	20 minutes
Haricot beans	20 minutes
Lentils - brown	15 minutes
- split red	15 minutes
Red kidney beans	20 minutes
Split peas	15 minutes

CHAPTER 9

SMALL COOKING EQUIPMENT

It would be very expensive for every kitchen to have every size baking sheet, cake tin, pie dish or basin. It would also take up a lot of space to store. So everyone has to be selective, and the main message is to buy the best you can afford and a selection in sizes according to your particular needs. Buy first the sizes you are going to need more often. Maybe you entertain a lot or have a large family, so the equipment you need will be larger than someone living on their own or who only cooks for two. Non stick tins and trays are more expensive, but with careful washing and avoiding scratching they last a long time and also aid towards a better cooked result. The extra cost when new can also be weighed against the cost of buying greaseproof paper, silicone paper and so on, often required to line other types of tins.

The majority of cake recipes suggest using between an 18 cm (7 inch) tin and a 23 cm (9 inch) tin so one or two around these sizes would be good to start with. If you have round tins and the recipe you want to make states a square tin, then to adapt it follow the chart on page 107.

If you already have equipment such as pudding basins measured in pints, and you wish to make a recipe given in metric measures you can easily find the metric capacity of the basins you have by following the information on page 110 – no need to rush out and buy new basins.

Vital for success is a good set of scales and measuring spoons.

BAKING TRAYS

Baking trays, sometimes called baking sheets, are used for baking biscuits, meringues, scones, Danish pastries or similar individual items of no fixed shape and no great depth. Often no particular size tray is required, but all the items to be cooked should fit easily onto the tray, allowing space for them to spread and rise as necessary. It is better to use a tray that is a bit too big than one where the items spread and join together during cooking. Before using, check that the tins will fit into your cooker, allowing some space around so that the hot air can freely circulate and provide an even temperature during cooking. Items cooked together on one baking sheet should be the same size and thickness to enable them to cook and brown evenly. In many recipes the recommended size of tray is given, sometimes in Imperial and sometimes in metric measures.

The most popular sizes of tray

Metric measurement				Imperial equivalent		
cm wide	cm long	cm deep		inches wide	inches long	inches deep
18	30.5	2	or	7	12	3/4
20.5	30.5	2	or	8	12	3/4
23	33	2	or	9	13	3/4
25.5	35.5	2	or	10	14	3/4

If the trays are not non-stick, then greasing may be suggested, or when making meringues or similar, a sheet of edible rice paper may be placed under the uncooked mixture and any of this that sticks to the food can be eaten. Otherwise a good non-stick lining paper to use is silicone.

Much larger trays are available but are only used commercially as they will not fit into the standard domestic cooker.

If you haven't a proper baking sheet do not make do with a tin with higher sides as this will prevent the hot air circulating evenly around the items during cooking. A flat underside of an upturned shallow pan may be able to be used instead.

SWISS ROLL TINS

If cooking a baked item such as a Swiss Roll it is vital to use the correct size tin with straight sides. Buy a proper Swiss Roll tin, do not make do with a baking tray. If the volume of mixture made is cooked in an incorrect sized tin then the finished product will either be too thin and overcooked or too thick and undercooked and will not roll.

Standard Basic Recipe for a Swiss Roll

100g (4oz) caster sugar
100g (4oz) plain flour
3 eggs

This should be cooked in a lined Swiss Roll tin measuring -
22.5 cm x 33.6 cm x 2 cm (9 in x 13 in x ¾ in)

This basic quantity of mixture should be baked at 220°C (425°F) (gas mark 7) for about 8 minutes until golden brown

To make a Chocolate Swiss Roll -

Replace 1 tablespoon (15 ml) of the flour in the above recipe with 1 tablespoon (15 ml) cocoa powder

Fillings for a Swiss Roll
For a cream filling use -

142 ml (¼ pint) double cream into which has been folded 2 teaspoons (10 ml) caster sugar and a few drops of vanilla essence.

For a butter cream filling use -

100 g (4oz) butter, creamed with 225 g (8oz) icing sugar plus a few drops of vanilla flavouring if desired.

CAKE TINS

To make a successful cake it is essential to use the correct size tin. Many tins aren't labelled at all by the manufacturers, while some are labelled in pints or litres to indicate their capacity. Others are measured in inches or centimetres, indicating the distance across the top of the tin, regardless of the depth or capacity. All this can be very confusing and lead to unsatisfactory results.

A good recipe should have been tested thoroughly and the size cake tin required written into the method. This is fine as long as the measures used are understood and the size of tins owned is known. Many recipes omit proper sizing information which can result in a cake which is out of proportion and undercooked or overcooked.

Too small a tin results in a cake which will rise higher than the edges of the tin and overflow. It will also be out of proportion and look too deep. Too large a tin results in the cake being too thin and shallow, causing it to cook too quickly and being likely to burn. The time the cake will take to cook will also vary according to the tin size used.

Every household cannot own a vast array of cake tins and trays of all shapes and sizes. But if you know how to calculate the quantity of mixture you are making and how to measure the size of a tin you own and wish to use, and how to adapt it, then there is no reason why a good result should not be achieved every time.

Measuring Cake Tins

A 20.5 cm / 8 inch square tin refers to the length of each side of the tin.

A 20.5 cm / 8 inch round tin refers to the diameter of the tin - the distance across the centre.

Approximate Imperial/metric equivalent of tin sizes

4 inch tin	is equivalent to a	10 cm tin
4½		11.5
5		13
5½		14
6		15
6½		16.5
7		18
7½		19
8		20.5
8½		21.5
9		23
9½		24
10		25.5
10½		26.5
11		28
11½		29
12		30.5

Swapping from square to round or round to square tins

You may have a recipe you want to make and it stipulates the size of the square tin you should cook it in. But if you want to make that recipe into a round cake what do you do. Or if the recipe states a round cake and you really want to make a square cake what do you do. Just refer to the chart below.

This shows for instance that if the recipe says use a 20.5 cm (8 inch) square tin then the mixture will fit well into a round tin 23 cm (9 inch) diameter.

Or if the recipe states a 28 cm (11 inch) round tin then you can use a 25.5 cm (10 inch) square tin instead to get a good result.

a square tin			a round tin	
inches	centimetres		inches	centimetres
5	13	can be substituted for	7	18
7	18		8	20.5
8	20.5		9	23
9	23		10	25.5
10	25.5		11	28
11	28		12	30.5
12	30.5		14	35.5

Cake tins in the shape of a number, a heart and so on are measured by their capacity.

To find the capacity of a tin

Fill it right to the very top with water. Carefully tip the water into a measuring jug and read the capacity from the scale on the side. Convert this information into litres or pints as necessary using the conversion chart on page 110.

To calculate how much cake mixture is required to fit in any given tin

- fill the tin with water to the depth you want the finished cake to be (loose bottomed tins should be lined with foil first!)

- transfer the water into a measuring jug

- make 680 g (1½ pounds) rich fruit cake mixture for every ½ litre (1 pint) water measured

- add together the weight of all the ingredients in the desired recipe to find the total weight of mixture and choose an appropriate tin that it will fit

- allow for a space about 2 cm (¾ inch) at the top as when the cake rises during cooking you do not want it to overflow the tin.

A rich fruit cake is usually cooked at 150°C (300°F) (Gas Mark 2).

A fruit cake cooked at this temperature will require these approximate baking times for the various tin sizes but a good recipe should tell you this.

square		round		capacity		cooking time in hours
ins	cm	ins	cm	pts	litres	
		5	13	1	½	2 - 2½
5	13	6	15	1½	¾	2½ - 3
6	15	7	18	2	1	3 - 3½
7	18	8	20	3	1¾	3½ - 4
8	20	9	23	4	2¼	4 - 4½
9	23	10	25	6	3½	6 - 6½
10	25	11	28	8	4½	7 - 7½

The above quantities and times cannot be precise but are a good standard average guide. Test the cake to see if it is cooked half an hour before you expect it to be ready and then check it again every ten to fifteen minutes until a thin bladed knife inserted into the middle of the cake comes out clean.

LOAF TINS
Loaf tins and large shallow tins in which to cook batters are measured by volume.

Miniature loaf tins
These are available for mini loaves. They measure approximately 9 cm x 7 cm x 4 cm (3½ inches x 3 inches x 1½ inches)

Small loaf tin
A standard small loaf weighs around 450 g or 1 pound

The approximate size of a small loaf tin is 20.5 cm long x 10 cm wide x 6.5 cm deep (8 ins long x 4 ins wide x 2½ ins deep) A tin of this size has a liquid capacity of around 1½ pints or 900 ml.

It is not usual to make one small loaf of bread on its own. Two small loaves can be produced from the quantities given below or they will make one large loaf.

Large Loaf Tin

A standard large loaf weighs around 900 grams or 2 pounds

This requires a tin size of 1¾ litre or 3 pints.

The approximate size of this tin is 23 cm long x 13 cm wide x 7 cm deep (9 ins x 5 ins x 3 ins). The amount of dough cooked in a tin of this size will be made from a standard recipe for a large loaf using -

700 g (1½ pound) strong plain flour
10 ml (2 level teaspoons) salt
15 g (½ oz) fresh yeast)
400 ml (¾ pint) water

Bread of course rises during baking, so when the dough is placed in the tin it should not fill it. It should only fill between half and three quarters of the tin. This is why the capacity of the tin suitable for the recipe you are making must be known.

Measuring a tin

If you have a tin and are not sure what size it is, follow the simple procedure given for the cake tin. Fill the tin to the brim with water, pour the water into a measuring jug and see how much liquid in litres or pints the tin will hold. Compare with the figures given above. This is useful to know even if you rarely make bread as many cakes are baked in a loaf shaped tin.

A tin is not lined when making bread, it is lightly greased, but if a loaf tin is used to cook a cake or pudding then line it or grease it according to the directions in the recipe.

PUDDING BASINS

Pudding basins are measured by the capacity they can hold, not by the width across the top or their depth. Do not be misled into thinking that the size of the basin is not important, and that using a large basin you have to hand for a small amount of mixture does not matter. If the correct size is not used, the pudding will not look in proportion, the cooking time may be wrong which will affect the texture and the pudding will look very strange when served. As with cakes, space must also be allowed for the pudding to rise.

Recipes often state 'transfer mixture to a 1 pint pudding basin', but they should now be made in metric measures and labelled in litre capacities. Unfortunately manufacturers rarely mark the capacity on a basin, but it is easy to work out the capacity of the basins you already possess or new ones if they are not labelled.

To find the metric capacity of a basin

Follow the instructions given for finding the capacity of a cake tin or loaf tin (see page 107) Read off how many litres, pints, or parts of a litre or pint your basin holds. Convert this information using the chart below.

¼	pint container holds	150 ml
½		300 ml
¾		450 ml
1		600 ml
1¼		750 ml (¾ litre)
1½		900 ml
1¾		1 litre
2		1.1 litre
2¼		1.3 litre
3		1.7 litre
4		2.2 litre
5		3 litre
6		3½ litre

Note - the volumes given are not exact conversions but are rounded up by the manufacturers.

If you wish to make a steamed pudding for four people from a basic recipe using -
100 g (4 oz) margarine
100 g (4 oz) caster sugar
2 eggs
175g (6 oz) self raising flour

this will require a pudding basin size 900 ml (1½ pint). Using this as a guide you can easily judge that you will require a 1.1 litre basin (2 pint) if the ingredients are increased half as much again to make a pudding for six people.

Size of saucepans for steaming

The depth and diameter of the saucepan used for steaming is important. You should be able to lift the basin in and out easily and safely and there should be adequate space around it for sufficient water to create the steam. Check all this before starting to mix the pudding. Remember to frequently check the level of water in the saucepan and top it up with boiling water when the level drops.

STANDARD SPOON MEASURES

In some recipes, exact measures of some ingredients are not required, they are added to suit the taste of the cook. However, in some cooking, when strong flavours are added, such as curry powder, careful measuring is required and this usually includes spoon measures.

There are many spoons which are not accurate measures although they are nice to own for their aesthetic appeal, such as coffee spoons or spoons in a canteen of cutlery. Just any old spoons, whether cheap or expensive, should not be used in the kitchen as they are not made to an accurate standard measurement.

Sets of measuring spoons are available at low cost from large department stores or kitchen suppliers. They are often made of plastic and each spoon should have its capacity stamped on the handle to avoid confusion. If they are not clearly marked do not buy them.

The information here refers to British equipment.

(For standard American and Australian spoon capacities see pages 56, 57 and 59)

Sets of UK spoons contain -
1 standard quarter teaspoon which holds 1.25 ml
1 standard half teaspoon which holds 2.5 ml
1 standard teaspoon which holds 5 ml
1 standard tablespoon which holds 15 ml
1 standard tablespoon is equivalent to 3 standard teaspoons

There is no such thing as a dessert spoon in cookery - a dessert spoon is what you eat your pudding with. If you find this written in a recipe then the nearest equivalent is 10 ml (2 teaspoons)

All printed recipes use *level* spoons unless otherwise stated. This fact is usually stated at the front of the book or recipe.

To get a level spoon, fill the spoon and level off the top surface by passing a knife across the top.

When measuring liquids by tablespoon the liquid finds its own level and does not need levelling off.

4 level tablespoons	=	1/8 UK pint	=	60 ml
6			=	90 ml
8		= 1/4 UK pint	=	100 ml

Standard measuring spoons in other countries vary so use of conversion charts will be necessary.

When some countries changed to the metric system in the 1970's, changes were made by each country independently. So where accuracy is required, refer to the appropriate conversion information for that country.

As standard spoons are needed to measure many things around the home and garden it is advisable to buy at least two sets - one for the kitchen and one to measure possible hazardous substances such as weed killer in the garden.

CHAPTER 10

LARGE KITCHEN EQUIPMENT
COOKERS

Cookers have changed beyond all recognition. Numerous varieties of ovens are in use, from older models still going strong, to more modern types which are automatic, self cleaning and so on.

Until a few years ago oven temperatures were nearly all marked in degrees Fahrenheit. The Fahrenheit scale is now rarely used in the UK and all temperatures are now given in degrees Celsius. But it is by no means everyone who has the most up-to-date automatic cooker and in other countries the Fahrenheit scale is still used. Many people have collections of old recipes and to enjoy these traditional favourites it is necessary to know how to convert temperatures given in degrees F to degrees C and gas mark.

Another problem is that in old recipes and even in some newer ones, the cooking instructions state 'cook in a cool oven' or 'cook in a moderate oven' or 'bake in a fairly hot oven' instead of giving an actual temperature figure. So what those terms mean and what the suggested oven temperature is for those descriptions has also been given. (See the conversion chart on page 115) Many people have gas ovens and the temperature equivalents for those are included.

Circotherm Cookers

The temperature of Circotherm cookers is marked on the Celsius (centigrade) scale. These cookers are more economical to use than other electric cookers as they cook at a lower temperature and are a bit quicker. Therefore if a recipe gives the temperature at which an item should be cooked as 180°C, (gas 4), those using a Circotherm cooker should set the dial at 160°C to cook the same item, as can be seen from the chart on page 115.

EQUIVALENT TEMPERATURE SETTINGS FOR COOKERS

Electric cooker Degrees Fahrenheit	Electric cooker Degrees centigrade	Circotherm cooker Degrees centigrade	Gas cooker Gas Mark	Heat of cooker
200	100	100	¼	very cool
225	110	110	½	very cool
250	130	120	½	very cool
275	140	130	1	cool
300	150	140	2	cool
325	160	150	3	very moderate
350	180	160	4	moderate
375	190	160	5	fairly hot
400	200	170	6	fairly hot
425	220	180	7	hot
450	230	190	8	very hot
475	240	190	9	very hot

Note - the temperatures shown are equivalent settings rather than exact conversions of degrees of heat.

Invest in an Oven Thermometer

Cookers are checked by the manufacturers before leaving the factory, but for good results it is wise to check the accuracy of the temperature of your cooker fairly regularly. An oven thermometer can be bought quite cheaply at hardware stores or the kitchen department of large department stores. Just place it in the oven on one of the shelves, not the bottom because the heating element is often there, and check that it reads the same as the oven dial just as the heat cuts out. For the best results, always consult the manufacturers instruction book that comes with your cooker.

COOKING IN A MICROWAVE COOKER

Microwave cooking is quick and straightforward but make sure you know the power of your machine and therefore the time and temperature required for each type of recipe as given in the manufacturers handbook. There are many different models of microwave cookers using different wattage and suggesting a wide range of temperatures, settings and timings according to whether the food is being de-frosted, heated through or cooked, or in some ovens grilled as well. It is impossible to list all variations for all models in this book so refer to the handbook for the use of your particular model.

REFRIGERATORS

The size of the refrigerator you choose will depend on the size of the family, your lifestyle, whether a lot of entertaining is done, the space you have available in the kitchen and the price you can afford pay. Never choose a fridge just because it looks attractive and fits in with your décor; it must be the correct model for the use to which it will be put. Refrigerators never seem big enough so it is wise to buy the biggest you can accommodate within your budget and space. Take the metric measurements of the height, width and depth of the space where you wish to place the fridge and take these to the shop. The external dimensions are important for checking that the fridge will fit in the kitchen but it is the internal measurement which tells you how much it will hold.

The capacity should be measured in litres but labels may also give the measurement in cubic feet. Approximate equivalent sizes are –

30 litres is approximately equivalent to 1 cubic foot.

100 litres	=	3.5 cubic feet
140 litres	=	5.0 cubic feet
180 litres	=	6.5 cubic feet
280 litres	=	10.0 cubic feet
340 litres	=	12.0 cubic feet
400 litres	=	14.0 cubic feet

Check carefully that the given size on the label in the shop shows the *net* capacity, that is the volume of *usable* space you will have to store things. There should also be information about the capacity of the freezer compartment.

A typical label will read –

Fresh food volume 159 litres

Frozen food volume 72 litres

Opening the door and looking at the inside of the fridge in the shop may look fine and the total capacity seem adequate, but if there is a salad compartment, maybe two, a freezer compartment and drinks section there may not be sufficient space remaining for the food you need to store in it. So think it through carefully.

Is the model you like energy efficient

It is well worth checking the energy efficiency of different models, after all it is the piece of equipment which will be on non-stop and using electricity all year round. The energy consumption is what it will use in kW/h per year and the various models can be compared by looking at the number given on the label. While this is a very helpful guide the actual consumption will vary a bit depending on how the appliance is used and where it is located. e.g. a fridge situated next to a cooker will have to work harder to keep the food inside it cool than one kept in a cool utility room.

For food safety it is very important that food is stored in the correct place and at the correct temperature in the refrigerator. Most have a 5 position adjustable thermostat with the numbers not actually indicating an exact temperature of degrees centigrade but are a guide. Read the manual which comes with your appliance to learn how you should set it. In summer time, or when a lot of food is being stored, or if the kitchen is hot because an oven is on, then a lower number setting should be used. Food poisoning organisms will not grow if they are colder than $4 - 5°C$ ($40 - 41°F$) while in a refrigerator, or at $-15°C$ ($5°F$) or colder in a freezer. Therefore the temperature of a refrigerator at home should be less than 4°C at all times. It is well worth buying a refrigerator thermometer because it is very important to check that items are being stored at the recommended temperature.

How to store food in a Refrigerator

Don't just pop any food inside anywhere without giving any thought.

Cold temperatures will not kill bacteria so it is important to stop them spreading from one food to another. Cover all food, but especially fresh, juicy foods and liquids. This will avoid contamination and the transfer of smells. Milk in particular picks up smells from other foods especially fruit such as strawberries.

Remember that the quality of food taken from a refrigerator is only as good as its quality when it went in. Make sure it is within its *'use by'* date. Don't leave leftovers in the fridge for several days and then when noone wants to eat them put them in the freezer. It is only sensible to store food that is good, fresh and uncontaminated. So eat it up in good time (see lists on pages 120 – 121 and wrap it suitably.

Raw Food

All food such as raw meat or fish which might drip blood or juices should be placed on the bottom shelf on a well covered plate or dish, then if drips do occur, no contamination is passed to foods placed under them which may not be cooked before eating.

Cooked Items and Baked Products

Place on the top and centre shelves.

Eggs

Many say that these are best not stored in a refrigerator but most models have a rack for them inside the door.

Butter and Margarine

Place in a covered plastic container or butter dish in the back of the door.

Cheese

Ideally this should not be stored in a fridge as it spoils its quality. If you do store it there due to lack of space elsewhere, make sure it is in a covered container and that you remove it to room temperature some while before being served. This is especially important if you have a selection of cheeses like brie or stilton varieties. Remember also that some cheeses are very pungent and this smell transfers easily to other foods in the fridge.

Salad Items

Store in the salad compartment at the bottom of the refrigerator. This area does not get quite so cold as the rest of the fridge. If the water in lettuce for instance gets too cold, ice is formed and the texture is ruined.

Milk and fruit juices

These should stay in their bottles or cartons in the back of the door.

Shortcrust pastry and similar items

This will store well in a tin after cooking but may be kept in a refrigerator for up to 3 months at the half way stage. Rub the fat into the flour and place it in a sealed polythene bag or polythene container with a tight lid. When you use it, weigh out 150g (6oz) of pastry mix for a recipe using 100 g (4oz) flour and add about 4 teaspoons of water.

Guide to Maximum Safe Storage Time for Foods in the Refrigerator

The following safe storage times presume that the refrigerator is at the recommended temperature and not higher than 4°C (40°F), that the food is fresh and within its *'use by'* date before storing.

Always check the label on any manufactured foods for any special storage advice.

Foods	How to Store	Recommended storage time
Dairy Foods		
Fresh milk	in a bottle or carton	3 - 4 days
Yogurt	as bought in a carton	follow 'use by' date
	if homemade	2 - 3 days
Butter and margarine	in their original wrappers	2 - 4 weeks
Cheese	in covered container	1 - 2 weeks depending on type and degree of ripeness when bought
Cream cheese	keep in covered container	5 - 7 days
Poultry		
Fresh	washed, wrapped in cling-film or foil	2 - 3 days
Cooked	cooled, wrapped, covered on a plate	2 - 3 days
Frozen	wrapped well and stored in the frozen food compartment unless it is to be defrosted and eaten within	2 - 3 days
Fish		
Raw	covered in a container or foil - store on lower shelf	1 - 2 days
Cooked	in a container or covered with foil	1 - 2 days

Foods	How to Store	Recommended storage time
Frozen	leave in shop packaging and place in frozen food compartment	follow instructions on packet
Meat		
Raw-all kinds	remove shop wrapping, wrap in foil or place in a covered dish. Store on lower shelves of refrigerator	
joints		3 days
small items like chops		3 days
mince and offal		1 day
sausages	wrap well	3 days
bacon	wrap well to prevent it drying out	7 - 9 days
Cooked meats		
	wrap well or place in covered dish on a higher shelf	3 - 4 days
Eggs	best bought in small quantities as needed and used within the date written on box	
whole yolks	cover with water in a cup	3 days
whites	store in covered container	3 - 4 days
hard boiled	leave in shell	7 days

After Food is Removed from the Refrigerator

Once food is removed from a refrigerator it should be eaten or cooked quickly. Care must be taken to prepare it and cook it in hygienic conditions. Once food reaches room temperature, bacteria become very active again and deterioration of the food starts. Keep raw and cooked food apart and use separate chopping boards and knives for each when preparing dishes.

FREEZERS

Choosing the Size of your Freezer

It is always recommended that one should buy the largest model one can afford and accommodate satisfactorily into the home. The capacity required will depend on whether the freezer is needed to store a lot of fresh produce from the garden and/or pick your own farms, or perhaps needs to accommodate lots of ready made frozen meals.

Positioning of the Freezer

A freezer must have space around it for warm air to escape from the condenser. It usually needs to be between 25 mm to 100 mm (1 inch to 4 inches) away from the wall. Unlike a refrigerator which needs to be to hand for frequent use, a freezer can be placed virtually anywhere. A dry, cool utility room or a well ventilated garage is ideal.

The Effect of Power Cuts on Frozen Food

Frozen food should keep in good condition for at least eight hours, longer if the weather is cold and if the door of the freezer is not opened. Try not to open the door for at least two hours after the power has been turned back on.

Capacity of Freezers

A rough guide is that you can store a total of 9 kg of frozen food per 30 litres or put another way 20 pounds of frozen food per cubic foot. The instruction book which comes with your freezer will indicate the cubic capacity of your freezer. More neat square packets or boxes of food can be stored as they can be packed closely together. Odd shaped bundles like joints of meat, or large packs of vegetables can take up a great deal of space as there will be a lot of air gaps in between. Other items like decorated cakes which require stiff covering and more head room can take up even more space. So the quoted figure is just a guide.

Buying Frozen Food

Frozen food should be the last items collected from the shelves when you are shopping, then placed straight from the shopping trolley into a cool bag for transportation home. Do not leave frozen foods in a shopping basket or boot of a car while other shopping is done or you stop somewhere for a cup of coffee. Get the food home and into the freezer first. Be sure to only buy what you are certain you can safely fit into your freezer at that time. The amount of food that can be home frozen at any one time varies from model to model so check the manufacturers instructions for this.

A rough guide is that 1 kilogram (about 2 pounds) of fresh food per cubic foot of freezer capacity can be frozen during any 24 hour period

Most freezer manufacturers suggest that not more than 10% of the capacity of the freezer should be added at any one time or the quality of the food already in the freezer may be affected by the temperature rising. If you know that a lot of food is going to be bought, turn the freezer to a colder setting before going shopping. This prevents the temperature of the freezer rising too high when a lot of cooler items are placed in it.

Certain foods such as ice-cream **must** stay frozen. **Do not** refreeze melted ice-cream. If meat defrosts then it should be cooked as a ready to eat dish such as a casserole, before replacing it in the freezer.

Packing Food

Whether large or small packs, wrap and label each separately before freezing. Do not try to economise by using plastic carrier bags from shops. Thick gauge polythene or freezer bags should be used for outer wrapping and should be securely fastened to be airtight. Thin polythene or cling film is suitable for separating items inside a larger thick bag. Plastic containers with airtight lids are excellent and are easy to stack. Well washed ice cream containers, yogurt pots and margarine tubs, all with lids, are useful for storing sauces or small items.

Ice cube trays are ideal for freezing baby foods, chopped herbs, condensed stock and so on which can then be removed individually as required.

How to Pack Individual items

You may wish to divide up some items before freezing. For instance if you have bought 1 kilogram (about 2 lbs) of mince you may wish to divide it into four, each packet then weighing 250 grams (about 8 ounces) which is about right for two portions if used in a spaghetti bolognese or similar dish. This means that you can use each small packet at a time without defrosting the whole lot .

Soups, stock and other liquids need to have a headspace in the container of 2.5 cm (1 inch) to allow them to expand during freezing.

Stews and casseroles also require headspace of 1cm (½ inch) and make sure there is plenty of liquid in the container so that all the contents are covered. To make serving easier and prevent having to be without good casserole dishes for a while, it is a good idea to line the dish with foil before cooking, then cook, cool and freeze it in the dish. When it is frozen, remove the foil parcel, label and store it, so freeing the dish for other use. Return it to the original dish when thawing and reheating for use. If reheating it in the microwave remember to remove the foil first.

Cakes are best decorated after defrosting but if they are decorated first then pack them in a rigid container with lots of headroom. Place a strip of strong foil under the cake so that it is easy to lift out of the container when frozen.

Labelling

You probably think you will remember what is in each package placed in the freezer. This is impossible. Once frozen it is often very difficult to tell what it is, so label with the contents, the number of servings or the amount and the date on which you have frozen it. Use packs in rotation using the longest stored first. Do not store for longer than the recommended time. (see chart on page 126) The food is unlikely to go bad but will certainly not taste good and the texture will almost certainly have deteriorated if kept too long.

Temperature of the Freezer

The home freezer should be minus 18°Celsius or below all the time. Although freezers should have the actual temperatures marked on the dial it is wise to invest in a freezer thermometer to check regularly that the temperature is accurate. Once food is removed from a freezer then care must be taken to defrost it thoroughly unless of course it is to be cooked from frozen such as some fish portions for instance. Once food reaches room temperature, bacteria become very active again and deterioration of the food starts, so it should be prepared and cooked quickly in hygenic conditions.

Storage Times for Food in a Freezer

Storage instructions along with nutritional information and the number of portions it will serve are usually given on bought packets. Given this information makes storage easy. But if you buy fresh food and freeze it yourself, or prepare a cooked dish, how long can it be safely frozen?

Freezing your Own Food

The chart on page 126 gives average times for storing food in a freezer providing that it is in a good, fresh, well prepared, clean state when put in the freezer, is wrapped correctly and when the temperature of the freezer is always at least minus 18°C.

The following list should be taken as a guideline. Some freezer manufacturers issue a handbook with more comprehensive lists.

	Months
Cooked meat - sliced	2
Casseroles - cooked	2
Cooked fish	1
Shellfish	1
White fish - raw	6
Oily or smoked fish – raw	2 - 3
Uncooked beef and lamb	12
Uncooked pork	3
Mince and sausages	2
Chicken and turkey - cooked	2
Bread	4 - 6
Small cakes and sponges	6
Rich fruit cake	9
Shortcrust pastry - raw	3
Shortcrust pastry – cooked	6
Sponge pudding - cooked	3
Vegetables - average	6 - 12 depending on type
Soft fruit	6
Stoned fruit	12
Egg whites and yolks – store separately	6
Ice cream	3
Hard cheese	4
Butter	4
Raw bacon - joint	6 weeks

Never refreeze thawed items unless they are cooked first e.g. frozen mince removed from the freezer, made into a dish and then refrozen.

Defrosting of food

This can be done at room temperature and is usually best done slowly in a cool place. Around 18°C (65° F) is best, out of direct sunlight. Or think ahead and defrost it in the refrigerator overnight prior to cooking. It can be defrosted in a microwave oven but this can often spoil the texture of the food.

Thawing Poultry

It is *very* important that *all* poultry and game is thoroughly defrosted before stuffing and cooking. One week before you want to eat a frozen turkey, check its weight and plan how long it will take to defrost. There will then be no last minute panic, or worse, a bird being put in the oven while it is still frozen inside. A kitchen is often too hot, especially if it is just before Christmas when the oven is on a lot and also central heating is on in the house. If possible a utility room or garage is often more suitable as long as the bird is clean and well covered.

Approximate time it takes to defrost frozen turkeys at room temperature or in a refrigerator

| Oven Ready Weight | | Thawing Time | |
kg	pounds	coolroom	refrigerator
1.5 - 2.25	3 - 5	20 hours	18 hours
2.75 - 3.0	6 - 7	30	30
3.6 - 4.0	8 - 9	36	48
4.5 - 5.0	10 -11	45	48
5.4 - 5.8	12 -13	48	60
6.3 - 7.7	14 -17	48	72
8.1 - 9.96	18 - 22	48	84
10.4 +	23+	48	96

Defrosting in a Microwave

Poultry can be defrosted in a microwave on a defrost cycle but it is advisable to check the manufacturers instructions first. Allow approximately 8 minutes per 450 g (per pound). Before relying on this method, check that any large bird such as a turkey will fit into your microwave with plenty of room for it to turn round.

Allow about 30 - 45 minutes standing time to complete the defrosting process.

Do not refreeze any part of the bird unless it is cooked first. This method is best only used in an emergency.

CHAPTER 11

MEASURING FOOD FOR ENERGY

While this book is concentrating on the measuring and weighing of food in the kitchen, it is relevant to include how the food is measured for its energy content. So many people want to lose weight and understand which foods are best avoided or only eaten in small quantities.

Several years ago it was decided in Britain that the Continental measure for dietary energy, the Kilojoule, should be used in place of the Kilocalorie as a unit of energy. However the British people continue to prefer the use of Kilocalories, commonly known as calories, to measure the energy they obtain from food and also to measure the energy their bodies use when performing various tasks.

Kilojoules as well as Kilocalories often appear on food labels in Britain. So it is helpful to be able to convert from one method to the other if you are counting the calories/joules in order to lose or gain weight or wish to compare the energy value of one food with another.

CONVERSION OF KILOCALORIES TO KILOJOULES AND MEGAJOULES

1 kilocalorie (kcal) equals 4.184 kilojoules (kJ).

For convenient quick reckoning this is usually rounded up to 4.2

So 1,000 kilocalories (kcal) equals 4,184 kilojoules or rounded up, equals 4,200 kilojoules (kJ).

By multiplying the number of calories by 4.2 the number of joules in the answer can be very large. To avoid working in such large numbers the megajoule can be used.

1 megajoule (MJ) equals 1,000 kilojoules (kJ) therefore 4,200 kilojoules can be written as 4.200 megajoules (MJ).

1 megajoule (MJ) also equals 239 kilocalories (kcal).

1 kilojoule (kJ) equals 0.239 kilocalories (kcal).

Calculating how many calories/joules you can eat

If you wish to follow a diet providing 2,200 kilocalories, this is how to work out how many kilojoules you can eat -

2,200 kilocalories multiplied by 4.2 equals 9,240 kilojoules

On a slimming diet of 1,150 kilocalories you can eat -

1,150 kilocalories multiplied by 4.2 equals a diet of 4,830 kilojoules.

If the daily amount of energy required is being calculated, then the calorie or joule content of all foods needs to be known. Booklets can be bought which give the calorie and kilojoule content of all foods.

On tins and packets of food the nutritional and energy content are almost always given in metric. So even if you prefer calculating in Imperial measures you will need to be familiar with metric measures to obtain this information. The amount may be written as the number of calories/joules in 100 g of the food or the calorie/joule content of one portion.

Energy obtained from Food

Calories or joules are obtained from the fat, carbohydrates, protein and alcohol in food.

1 gram of fat	supplies 9 kilocalories	or 37 kilojoules
1 gram of alcohol	supplies 7 kilocalories	or 29 kilojoules
1 gram of carbohydrate	supplies 4 kilocalories	or 17 kilojoules
1 gram of protein	supplies 4 kilocalories	or 17 kilojoules

DO YOU NEED TO LOOSE WEIGHT?

The size of the waist circumference is a good indicator of the overall health risk.

Excess fat which is deep down in the region of the stomach gives a large waist circumference and an '*apple*' shape.

Excess fat found under the skin, around the bottom, hips and thighs gives a smaller waist circumference resulting in a '*pear*' shape. This is generally accepted to be less harmful to health but is also best removed by diet and/or exercise.

BODY MASS INDEX

The Body Mass Index (BMI) is the one main way of assessing whether you are really overweight or not. A few years ago a height/weight chart for a light, medium or large frame could be used as a quick guide and this can still be very useful. But this does not take into account muscle or bone weight or what percentage of the total weight is body fat. The BMI provides a more reliable picture and is the one used by doctors.

It is calculated by dividing the weight of the body in kilogrammes by the square of the height in metres. Sometimes it is referred to as the Quartlet Index.

To calculate your Body Mass Index

It may sound daunting but is straight forward, especially if you have a calculator!

First weigh yourself carefully in kilograms. Then measure your height in metres. You can do the latter by standing up straight against a wall *without any shoes on* and asking a friend to make a mark on the wall exactly level with the top of your head. Then measure from the mark to the floor in metres.

Next, divide your weight in kg by your height squared in metres.

How do you do that ?

If you weigh for instance 65 kg and your height is 1.6 metres you do this sum.

Multiply your height by your height to square it e.g. 1.6 x 1.6 = 2.56

Divide this figure into your weight

65 ÷ 2.56 = 25.4

Refer to the text below and you will see that you are just slightly overweight.

By using this system of measure it is easier to define correctly the various grades of obesity.

A BMI of between 20 and 24.9 is regarded as normal and indicates that you have no excess fat in or around the body. A BMI above this indicates that steps should be taken to loose weight.

If your BMI is	20	you are underweight
BMI	20 - 24.9	you are within normal range
BMI	25 - 29.9	plump or Grade 1 obesity
BMI	30 - 39.9	moderately overweight or Grade 11 obesity
BMI	40	severe obesity or Grade 111 obesity

INDEX